Peter the Great

LANCASTER PAMPHLETS

Peter the Great

Stephen J. Lee

London and New York

For Max and Joan

First published 1993
by Routledge
11 New Fetter Lane, London EC4P 4EE

Simultaneously published in the USA and Canada
by Routledge
29 West 35th Street, New York, NY 10001

Reprinted 1996

First Published in hardback 2001

Routledge is an imprint of the Taylor & Francis Group

© *1993 Stephen J. Lee*

Typeset in 10/12pt Bembo by
Ponting–Green Publishing Services, Chesham, Bucks
Printed in Great Britain by
TJ International Ltd, Padstow, Cornwall

British Library Cataloguing in Publication Data
A catalogue record for this book is available from the British Library

Library of Congress Cataloging in Publication Data
Lee, Stephen J.
Peter the Great / Stephen J. Lee.
p. cm. – (Lancaster pamphlets)
Includes bibliographical references
1. Russia – History – Peter I, 1689-1725
I. Title. II. Series
DK131.L44 1993
947'.05'092 – dc20 92–44016 CIP
ISBN 0–415–09279–5 (pbk)
ISBN 0–415–26861–3 (hbk)

Contents

v

Foreword

Lancaster Pamphlets offer concise and up-to-date accounts of major historical topics, primarily for the help of students preparing for Advanced Level examinations, though they should also be of value to those pursuing introductory courses in universities and other institutions of higher education. Without being all-embracing, their aims are to bring some of the central themes of problems confronting students and teachers into sharper focus than the textbook writer can hope to do; to provide the reader with some of the results of recent research which the textbook may not embody; and to stimulate thought about the whole interpretation of the topic under discussion.

Illustrations

Maps

Figures

Plates: images of Peter the Great

Chronological outline of the reign of Peter the Great

1
The setting

The approach: an explanation

This pamphlet examines the contribution of Peter I (1682–1725) to the development of Russia. It considers the relationship between the man and the environment in which he lived – and the extent to which each of these influenced the other. Because of the sheer power of his personality, Peter has been the subject of numerous studies and it would be as well at the outset to establish the basic approach to be taken here.

One possibility would be to accept the emphasis, common to the nineteenth century, on the overriding importance of great men in determining events. The Russian historian, Soloviev (1820–79), argued that Peter was personally responsible for directing the evolution of Russia into an entirely new channel of his own devising, for which he can justly be called 'the greatest leader of history, for no one can claim a place of higher significance in the history of civilization' (Raeff 1963: p. 82). This approach, however, ascribes too much importance to personal influence and fails to acknowledge that leaders can also be creatures of circumstances or that at least some of their work withers away after their death.

At the opposite extreme is the Marxist conception of history as the inexorable working through of economic forces in the form of class conflict, the agents of which are the great men

1

who emerge, as they are needed, from their environment. This explanation is also inadequate, since determinist writing rarely provides a convincing explanation for the full range of human achievement.

Modern biographers consciously avoid both of these approaches and aim to achieve a more balanced perspective. They would most probably agree with A. L. Rowse that

> the most congenial, as well as the most concrete and practical, approach to history is the biographical, through the lives of the great men whose actions have been so much part of history, and whose careers in turn have been so moulded and formed by events.
>
> (A. L. Rowse quoted in Sumner 1950: General introduction)

In this way, 'a biography of a great man' can be used 'to open up a significant historical theme'.

Even this approach, however, has its problems. In adopting an individual leader as the focus, the biographer tends to concentrate on the details relating to that individual, usually at the expense of an analysis – in equivalent detail – of more impersonal trends. One means of countering the imbalance which this creates was suggested by Sir Lewis Namier. Biography should be diversified as much as possible, enabling a detailed view of a particular period of history to be built up through a study of as many as possible of the characters involved in it. But this presents a practical problem; the result of such a method would be voluminous, always supposing, in our case, that there were sufficient source material available on the other personalities in Peter's reign.

A brief analysis of Peter the Great cannot, therefore, be any of these things. This study attempts, instead, to cover both the personal importance of Peter the Great and the broader trend of developments in seventeenth- and eighteenth-century Russian history. It draws, in the process, on material from three main types of secondary source referred to in the Bibliography: general histories of Russia, biographies of Peter the Great, and more detailed monographs on specific subjects. Extracts are drawn from these to illustrate the divergence of views on most of the issues covered.

The reign: an outline

Peter was the outstanding member of the early Romanov dynasty, his predecessors having been Michael (1613–45), Alexis I (1645–76), and Theodore III (1676–82).

His youth was marked with upheaval and violence which left a lasting imprint on his character. On the death of Theodore III, a struggle for power occurred between the two leading aristocratic fractions, each of which tried to impose its own nominee as successor to the throne. The Naryshkins backed Peter, who was proclaimed Tsar in 1682. The Miloslavsky group, however, preferred Peter's feeble-mined half-brother, Ivan. Within weeks of Peter's accession, they encouraged a revolt of the Streltsy, or palace guard, which resulted in bloodshed and horror personally witnessed by Peter at the tender age of 10. The outcome was that Peter and Ivan were declared joint rulers. In reality, power fell increasingly into the hands of Ivan's sister, Sophia. Peter was exiled with his mother to Preobrazhenskoye, where he received little formal education but showed interest in foreign influences acquired from a nearby German quarter, or colony. His fortunes changed in 1689 when Sophia was removed from power in another palace coup and placed in the Novodevichy convent. Peter finally came into his own in 1694, going on to assume sole and undisputed control on the death of his brother Ivan in 1696.

Having been so long frustrated by this tortuous route to power, Peter now exploded into action. His immediate priority was to seize from Turkey an outlet to the Black Sea. This was accomplished with the capture in 1696 of Azov on the River Don. Then, conscious of the backwardness of his country, Peter invested over a year of his reign in travel abroad. In 1697 he embarked on a 'Great Embassy' to several western countries, including the Dutch Republic and England. He acquired a wide range of technical knowledge and expertise, sending tools and instruments back to Russia for future imitation. As Peter was on the point of heading for Venice in 1698, news came of a revolt in Moscow by the Streltsy regiment, who were planning to take over the government and the capital. He returned immediately to Russia, succeeded in crushing the uprising and exacted the most bloody and brutal revenge on the insurgents. The contrasting extremes of his character are nowhere more clearly shown than in this year of his reign.

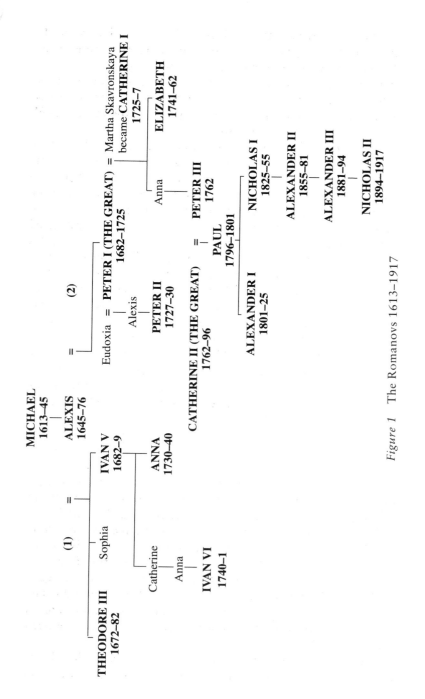

Figure 1 The Romanovs 1613–1917

Now secure from internal disorder, Peter was able to turn his attention to the twin themes of expanding and modernizing Russia. His intention was to open a 'window on the west'. In a literal sense, this involved taking – by force – an outlet in the Baltic to open regular trade routes with western Europe. Metaphorically, it meant reforming and updating Russia's political, military and economic institutions.

The themes of expansion and diplomacy are dealt with in Chapter 2. In 1700 he diverted his resources from the struggle with Turkey, involving himself instead in the Great Northern War in Sweden, the main obstacle to Russian expansion in the Baltic. Taking advantage of the preoccupation of most of Europe with the War of the Spanish Succession, he constructed with Saxony, Poland and Denmark a coalition against Charles XII of Sweden. In the first year of the war, however, Peter's army was routed by the Swedes at Narva and the road to Moscow lay open. Fortunately for Peter, Charles XII chose not to press home his advantage. Instead, he moved westwards against Poland and Saxony and, for the following six years, gave Russia the respite Peter so desperately needed.

It was not until 1707 that Charles turned his attention back to Russia, by which time Peter had extended his hold on the Baltic, constructed a new capital, St Petersburg, and introduced extensive military changes (covered in pp. 40–3). Over the following year Charles's invading army was drawn ever deeper into the Ukraine, eventually to be defeated by the Russians at Poltava in May 1709: the reasons for this are explained on pp. 19–23. Peter fared less well in a subsequent attempt to invade Turkey, agreeing in 1711 to surrender all his previous gains in the south, including Azov (see pp. 26–9). In striking contrast to this, his successes continued in the North as he overran a large part of Finland and inflicted a crushing naval defeat in 1714 on the Swedes at Cape Hango. The end of the Great Northern War came in 1721 with the Treaty of Nystadt by which Russia acquired vital areas which gave Russia permanent access to the Baltic (p. 24). During this last decade of his reign Peter had also sought further expansion in Asia, especially in eastern Siberia and the Caspian Sea area (see pp. 29–31).

The demands of war placed intolerable burdens on the administrative and economic fabric of Russia. Using the information and knowledge derived from the West, Peter proceeded to update his country's institutions and infrastructure. He gave priority to military reforms (pp. 40–4), establishing a national army, which was recruited by a general levy and equipped with uniforms and the most advanced forms of weapons, as well as Russia's first navy. The impetus of war brought extensive administrative reform, including a senate and nine administrative colleges at the centre (pp. 44–51) and a partially reshaped provincial government (pp. 51–4).

The conflict with Sweden also promoted rapid industrialization (pp. 54–7), especially the development in the Urals of the iron industry, manufactories and foundries. At the same time, commerce with western Europe was stimulated; contracts were clearly assisted by the acquisition of the Baltic lands from Sweden. On the other hand, agriculture scarcely benefited from Peter's modernization programme, remaining essentially backward and set into a rigid social structure which further depressed the conditions of the serfs. The nobility were granted extensive social privileges, in return for which they surrendered to the central authority some of their political influence. Peter also introduced a series of religious changes (pp. 61–4), the basic intention of which was to reduce the Church to the status of a government department and to make more effective use of its resources.

Peter's death in 1725 was followed by a series of short reigns until the accession of Catherine the Great; these successors were Catherine I (1725–7), Peter II (1727–30), Anna (1730–40), Ivan VI (1740–1), Elizabeth (1741–2), and Peter III (1762). A theme emphasized throughout the pamphlet is that this period tested the effectiveness of Peter's changes and whether or not Peter's title 'the Great' was deserved in the longer term, an issue considered in Chapter 4.

The personality

It was customary for seventeenth- and eighteenth-century rulers to live in splendour in magnificent royal courts. The largest of these was Versailles, which had been established by Louis XIV as a means of keeping his troublesome nobility within a 'gilded cage', an example followed by most of his contemporaries.

There, however, the rulers themselves became imprisoned, having to observe a complex daily ritual and dominated by the details of formal etiquette. Much the same had already happened in Moscow within the walls of the Kremlin, even though this had been punctuated by the occasional eruption of violence.

It required a particularly strong personality to rise above courtly minutiae and consciously to promote changes and reforms. An instant advantage would be an imposing physical appearance which could intimidate all those within immediate contact. Peter I was just under seven feet tall and immensely powerful and vigorous. According the French courtier, the Duc de Saint-Simon, who met him in France in 1717:

> The Czar was a very tall man, exceedingly well made; rather thin, his face somewhat round, a high forehead, good eyebrows, a rather short nose, . . . rather thick lips, large, bright, piercing and well open; his look majestic and gracious when he liked, but when otherwise, severe and stern.
>
> (Raeff 1963: p. 10)

He could also inspire sheer terror through his fits of violent temper in which he resorted to kicks and blows. Usually such a transformation was signalled in advance. According to Saint-Simon there was 'a twitching of the face . . . which appeared to contort his eyes and all his physiognomy, and was frightful to see'; this 'gave him a wild and terrible air' which was guaranteed to inspire panic and instant compliance with whatever order Peter chose to issue.

Because of the unquestioned personal ascendancy he established over those who served him, Peter could give free rein to his personal eccentricities. Spurning the ceremonial which traditionally surrounded the tsars, he abandoned the Kremlin, cut the size of his retinue and reduced the royal stables by 3,000 horses. He nearly always wore old clothes and shoes, rarely sported the customary wig and never, except in winter, a hat. His meals were massive and frequent, and were consumed usually without utensils and often without plates. His preferred companions were artisans and merchants and he had strong liking for hard manual labour; during his visit to western Europe in 1697, for example, he joined the workers of the Dutch East India Company in the Oostenburg shipyards.

Peter was also able to pursue unimpeded a wide range of unorthodox interests and commitments. He was fascinated by all mechanical devices and developed a variety of practical talents as stonemason, turner of wood and ivory, bookbinder and blacksmith. In Holland he studied science under Boerhaave and Leeuwenhoeke and mechanics under van der Heyden, while learning the rudiments of architecture from Schynvoet and military engineering from van Coehorn. He even turned his hand to dentistry – and to his courtiers' teeth. Such enthusiasm was instinctive and untutored: after all, his schooling had been interrupted by his stormy youth and temporary exile to Preobraz-henskoye. He was thereby liberated from the constraints of tradition which would have been imposed by a formal education. He fully intended that all visible manifestations of western progress were to be imprinted on to Russia, by force if necessary, when and where the opportunity arose. He lacked the perspective and sensitivity which might have stayed his hand from cutting into the fabric of traditional Russia. Two descriptions have been provided by biographers which, when combined, provide a powerful image. V. Klyuchevsky calls Peter the 'artisan Tsar', aptly summarizing his priorities, while M. S. Anderson encapsulates his methods in the term 'iconoclast'.

Such epithets have to be seen in the context of another of Peter's characteristics – an inexhaustible capacity for hard work and perseverance. He never spared himself in implementing the changes he regarded as essential for his country, and he expected similar devotion and commitment from his subjects. He expended millions of his subjects in the pursuit of modernization and expansion but, as he pointed out, 'I have not spared and I do not spare my life for fatherland and people'. According to Lentin:

> Peter was both the agent and symbol of change . . . he was above all a man of action. . . . People to him were little more than cogs in a machine, functional and expendable; in his fervour for change he spared no one, himself least of all.
>
> (Lentin 1973: ch. 1)

He was even prepared to throw his own resources into the balance, handing over to the state treasury personal estates of nearly 30,000 acres and 50,000 houses which had brought in a huge personal revenue.

So far Peter's personality has been portrayed as uncouth and obsessive but also as innovative and constructive. There is, however, a darker side. Russia was civilized by a man who himself behaved like a barbarian.

At times this was relatively trivial, little more than a transgression beyond the normally acceptable bounds of eccentricity. For example, he repaid the hospitality of Sir John Evelyn in 1697 by ruining his house at Deptford, permitting his retinue to slash the paintings, burn the furniture and flatten the gardens. In Russia he was similarly gross, surrounding himself with dwarfs or making courtiers eat live tortoises for some minor transgression. He also drank heavily and established the Holy Synod of Fools and Jesters as a grotesque mockery of the ritual of the Church.

More serious was the reputation he earned for cruelty. This was particularly apparent in the way he punished the Streltsy for their revolt in 1697. Over a thousand of those involved were put through torture chambers to be crippled and maimed, before being beheaded, or hanged, or cut to pieces inch by inch, or broken on the wheel and allowed to die in agony. Another example was Peter's treatment of his son in 1718. Peter strongly disapproved of Alexis, eventually disinheriting him in favour of a younger half-brother. Worse was to follow as Alexis was put on trial for treason. The judicial process involved the use of torture – personally supervised by Peter – under which Alexis died.

This clearly shows a major defect within Peter's personality, but the precise form has been the subject of controversy. M. T. Florinsky refers to Peter as 'savagely cruel'. According to W. Durant: 'Peter's almost personal massacre of the Streltsi suggests a sadistic pleasure in cruelty, an orgasm of blood' (Durant 1963: ch. 13). Massie, however, disagrees. While there is no doubt that Peter was personally present during interrogations and executions, 'He did not enjoy seeing people tortured. . . . He tortured for practical reasons of state: to extract information. To him these were natural, traditional and even moral actions' (Massie 1981: ch. 19). Peter applied the judicial procedure to Alexis as 'the final, legal step required in his legitimate defence of the state and his life work. That it was prompted by political necessity rather than personal rancour he felt was obvious' (Massie 1981: ch. 54). M. S. Anderson agrees:

he showed little deliberate brutality, no taste for cruelty. . . .
The sufferings he inflicted on tens of thousands of humble
and helpless people he never desired for their own sake. They
were the inevitable result of his efforts to wrench Russia out
of what he saw as stultifying conservatism and humiliating
weakness. As such they had to be accepted and enforced. But
they were always incidental to his real objectives.

(Anderson 1978: ch. 7)

All the same, Peter's bloodletting went well beyond conventional bounds in a Europe which was entering the Enlightenment. While other countries were tempering autocracy with
rationalism, Peter was becoming more and more arbitrary and
obsessive. Although his intention was to drag Russia into the
European mainstream, and to do so by flouting Russian tradition, he nevertheless employed methods which were similar to
the worst excesses of his notorious ancestor, Ivan the Terrible
(1533–84). In this respect, at least, there is some truth in the
impression formed by Sophia Charlotte, Electress of Hanover
in 1697: 'He is a prince at once very good and very bad; his
character is exactly that of his country.' It is also no co-
incidence that Joseph Stalin, who combined all the ruthlessness
of Peter and the paranoia of Ivan, saw himself as the natural
heir to both.

How was Peter perceived visually? The best-known images of
Peter were produced by western artists or sculptors. The earliest
are two English impressions made in 1698 during Peter's Great
Embassy to the West. Sir Godfrey Kneller's portrait (plate 1)
showed Peter at the age of 25, in a typically western pose, with
the fleet he was in the process of creating in the background. In
Faithorne's engraving of the same year (plate 2) Peter's features
bore a close resemblance to Kneller's version, but his dress is, in
complete contrast, traditionally Muscovite. During his second
visit to the West in 1717 portraits of Peter, then aged 44, were
commissioned from Aert de Gelder, Carl Moor (plate 5) and J.
M. Nattier. These show Peter in maturity with the effect of his
labours clearly etched into his features, although the settings
again vary. By the time of his death in 1725 his appearance had
changed considerably. Excessive drinking and the prolonged
impact of syphilis and urinary infections weakened his body and
bloated his face, as shown in the waxwork depicted on plate 6.

This bears a striking resemblance to the death-mask taken after his final illness. But perhaps the finest representation of Peter was Serov's painting nearly 200 years later (plate 8). This focuses on Peter's most abiding qualities – restlessness and energy – before they were dulled by exhaustion and disease.

2

War, conquest and diplomacy

Russia before Peter the Great: expansion and stagnation

When Peter came to the throne Russia was ready to take on a more significant and assertive role in European affairs after a long cycle of expansion, collapse and recovery.

The record of expansion extended far back into the Middle Ages. The earliest conquests were accomplished by the principality of Novgorod as a result of the campaigns of its thirteenth-century ruler, Alexander Nevski. Novgorod, in turn, was incorporated into the principality of Muscovy during the reign of Tsar Ivan III (1462–1505). Ivan the Terrible (1533–84) pushed Muscovy's territory westwards, at the expense of Poland and the Ukraine, and eastwards with the conquest of Tartar areas such as Kazan and Astrakhan. By the time of Ivan's death Muscovy had extended beyond the Urals and, although as yet only one-third of the size she was eventually to become, Russia was already the largest state in Europe.

Then the momentum ceased and, for a while, the frontiers actually contracted. The main reason was that between 1584 and 1613 Muscovy experienced a period of internal upheaval. Part of the problem was that Ivan the Terrible had murdered his son and heir which meant a disputed succession and a series of weak and manipulatable tsars. The feeble-minded Fedor I (1584–98) fell under the influence of his brother-in-law, Boris

Godunov, who had himself elected to the throne in 1598. The situation deteriorated rapidly between 1605 and 1613 during the so-called *smutnoe vremia*, or 'time of troubles'. Fedor II was murdered by the boyars, or nobility, in 1606 and the political vacuum in Muscovy attracted the attention of two major powers: Poland to the west and Sweden to the north. The Poles backed two pretenders to the throne, financing an invasion by one Dimitry in 1604 and another in 1608. The only way in which Vasili Shuiski, the successor to Fedor II, could deal with this threat from Poland was to seek the assistance of Sweden, signing away in exchange Muscovy's hold on the shores of the Gulf of Finland. It was not until 1612 that the Poles were finally evicted from the Kremlin and, with the coronation of Michael Romanov the following year, Muscovy was at last able to begin the process of territorial reconstruction. This proved both arduous and expensive, and met with very mixed results.

The balance sheet was at least partly in Muscovy's favour. She more than held her own against Poland, succeeding in 1654 in transferring the eastern part of the Ukraine from Polish to Russian sovereignty; M. T. Florinsky goes so far as to say that this was the 'most important single feature of Russia's territorial expansion in the seventeenth century'. More extensive, at least in terms of area, was the spread of Russian rule across Siberia, in the wake of trade and commercial expansion. The revival of expansionism was accompanied by a consciousness among seventeenth-century tsars of the need to modernize in order to avoid a possible return to isolation, backwardness, weakness and foreign aggression. Their changes therefore included the foundation of the Tula armaments works in 1632 and the import of foreign mercenaries and foreign advisers, the latter amounting to almost 20,000 before the accession of Peter the Great.

On the debit side, the seventeenth-century tsars made very little progress against two of the powers which hemmed in Muscovy: Sweden and Turkey. The only real success was Michael's recapture of Novgorod from the Swedes in 1617. Alexis, however, failed in the Russo-Swedish war of 1656–61 to regain the Gulf of Finland. This meant that Muscovy still had no access to the Baltic, something that it was very much in Peter's mind to redress when he came to power. The seventeenth-century tsars also failed to break through to the Black Sea in the

Map 1 The expansion of Russia under Peter the Great in historical perspective

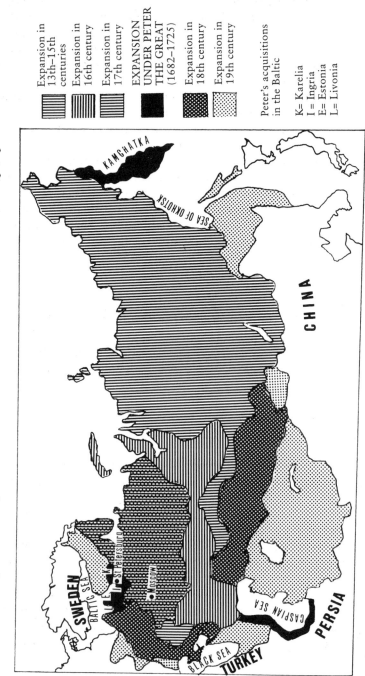

Expansion in
13th–15th
centuries

Expansion in
16th century

Expansion in
17th century

EXPANSION
UNDER PETER
THE GREAT
(1682–1725)

Expansion in
18th century

Expansion in
19th century

Peter's acquisitions
in the Baltic

K= Karelia
I = Ingria
E= Estonia
L= Livonia

south, despite attempts by Fedor III (1676–82) and the regent Sophia (1682–9) to join with other powers in attacking Turkey; the failure of the campaigns against the Crimean Tartars in 1687 and 1689 left Peter with another set of unfinished business. Even the momentum for modernization was difficult to sustain, largely because of the powerful opposition exerted by the Orthodox Church. Western influences undoubtedly existed but were considered potentially corrupting. This explains their confinement to the German Quarter, with which Peter had such extensive contacts in his early days.

Overall, the influence Muscovy could hope to exert in European affairs was as yet limited. According to the philosopher, Descartes, she was considered to be of less importance than the smallest German principality of the Holy Roman Empire. And yet the momentum of recovery was about to be sustained – and intensified. This was made possible partly by objective circumstances which favoured Russia and partly by the timely intervention of powerful individual leadership.

Objective factors favouring further Russian expansion

Russia burst on to the European scene at the beginning of the eighteenth century largely because the scene itself had changed. A hundred years earlier three states had taken advantage of Muscovy's crisis and had dominated eastern Europe. Now these three states were themselves in varying stages of crisis and decline and there was scope for a new power to fill the vacuum left by their contraction.

The most dangerous, but also the most vulnerable, was Sweden. She had reached a military peak during the Thirty Years' War and had benefited territorially from the Peace of Westphalia in 1648. Increasingly, however, her new German possessions brought her into conflict with Brandenburg, at whose hands she suffered a humiliating defeat at the Battle of Fehrbellin in 1675. When Charles XII came to the throne in 1697, he inherited a kingdom with a much larger history and sense of importance than its small economic base and tiny population warranted. The Swedish Empire was basically artificial, consisting in the south of coastal enclaves which could be maintained only by a military presence. Charles XII started his reign with a series of spectacular victories, but Sweden lacked the economic infrastructure to sustain these indefinitely. The time was therefore ripe for Russia to start dismantling Sweden's southern littoral.

Poland's decline was more obvious. She had been severely weakened after 1650 by a series of wars with Sweden, Brandenburg and Turkey, suffering extensive devastation and heavy population loss. She also experienced internal problems. Ever since the end of the Jagellon line in 1572 Poland had possessed an elective rather than an hereditary monarchy. Although this could produce outstanding rulers like John Sobieski (1674–96), it was more likely to result in a powerful monarchy being replaced by a divided oligarchy. But all this had an effect which was very different from that of Swedish decline. Poland was less immediately attractive to Russia than were Sweden's Baltic territories, which meant that by and large Peter did not take advantage of Poland's weakness. But those – like Charles XII – who did, found themselves in a morass of complex politics and diplomacy which absorbed an enormous amount of resources and energy. Russia therefore benefited from an over-extended Sweden being bogged down in an anarchic Poland.

The Ottoman Empire had passed the zenith it had reached in the sixteenth century under Suleiman the Magnificent. This was due partly to the declining quality of the Sultanate between 1566 and 1695 and partly to a series of defeats at the hands of Austria and the Holy Roman Empire at St Gothard (1664), Khoczim (1673), Lemburg (1675), Vienna (1683), Mohacs (1687) and Zenta (1697). Turkey's decline was less precipitate than that of Sweden, which had outgrown its own strength, or Poland, which had collapsed inwards. Instead, Turkey became introverted and aimed at conserving what it still possessed. This, too, was an advantage to Russia since Turkey was unlikely, as a satiated power, to be tempted into sudden forays against Russian territory. This meant that the initiative and choice of action now lay with Moscow.

How much better, therefore, was the prospect facing Peter in 1693 than that which confronted his grandfather, Michael, in 1613. The crucial questions were whether Peter would seize his opportunity, and if so what he would make his priorities.

Positive leadership was vital if Russian expansion was to be maintained. Peter's commitment was total, both to the military campaigns and to the modernization of Russia's infrastructure to support them. His impact on Russia was enormous. He took full advantage of the opportunities Russia had at the end of the seventeenth century, although it is difficult to see what headway he could have made had these advantages not existed. Much of his policy was based on trial and error and he seemed to lack an overall blueprint for expansion; occasionally he even committed a serious blunder. Overall, however, he developed four major objectives.

One was to gain access to the Baltic to win back territories lost to Sweden in the seventeenth century and to open up a window on to the west. The recapture of Ingria and Karelia was Peter's main aim and dominated his reign to such an extent that it also dictated the pattern and pace of most of his domestic reforms.

A second objective was to break through to the Black Sea at the expense of the Ottoman Empire. This was chronologically to be his first target, although he came to accept after the Azov campaigns that it was of secondary importance and that the full weight of Russian resources should be brought to bear in the struggle against Sweden.

Third, he proposed to complete the internal expansion which had occurred during the seventeenth century and to ensure the subjection of over 100 linguistic and ethnic groups which were now part of his empire. The main directions of expansion were southwards along the coastline of the Caspian Sea and eastwards across the Bering Strait in search of new territory in a third continent. All this was very much within the traditional mode of expansion but, again, was subordinated to the war in the Baltic.

Finally, he aimed to put Russia on the diplomatic map of Europe and reverse the humiliating lack of consultation she had experienced during the course of the seventeenth century. Peter did not, however, distinguish between diplomacy and conflict, which meant that raising Russia's diplomatic prestige would be the inevitable result of her emergence as a great military power.

The conflict with Sweden 1700–21

In 1699 Peter drew up an alliance with Augustus II, Elector of Saxony and King of Poland, and Frederick IV of Denmark. The target was Charles XII of Sweden with whom Peter had previously agreé, by the Treaty of Kardis, to remain at peace. This *volte face* was all the more unexpected as Peter had not completed his task in the south; although he had captured the port of Azov in 1697, he had not accomplished his proposed conquest of the Crimea. The fact, however, that Peter was forgoing the opportunity to turn the knife in Turkey indicates that his real priority was to take advantage of the promise of easier pickings in the north. It is probable that Peter considered that Sweden was more immediately vulnerable and exploitable than Turkey and that he could resume Russian ambitions in the south at a later date. In the meantime he had the chance to regain Russia's lost Baltic lands and destroy forever the legend of Swedish military power. There is even evidence that he hoped to overthrow the Swedish monarchy in favour of a republic, since republics were 'less dangerous to their neighbours'.

The coalition was, however, devastated by the speed and effectiveness of the Swedish response to the Danish capture of Gottorp, the Saxion invasion of Livonia and the Russian siege of Narva. Charles picked off his enemies in 1700, eliminating Denmark first and then inflicting a crushing defeat on a numerically superior Russian force at Narva. How can this initial disaster for Russia be explained?

One of the reasons was the defectiveness of Russia's war effort at this stage. Peter's declaration of war on Sweden was entirely premature, since Russian troops were less disciplined and experienced than the Swedes; according to one of the foreign commanders who served Peter at Narva they 'ran about like a herd of cattle, one regiment mixed up with another, so that hardly twenty men could be got into line' (Massie 1980: ch. 25). The officers were incompetent, and this included the commander-in-chief at Narva, Prince Carl Eugene de Croy. Peter's own record at Narva was far from exemplary, as he fled from the battle and went into hiding. The Swedes were a complete contrast. Charles XII acted with precision and speed, detaching Denmark first by a swift landing, which, by the Peace of Travendal, forced Frederick to pull out of the coalition.

Having naval control over the Baltic, Charles was then able to transport his army to the Gulf of Riga. He brilliantly exploited the element of surprise and the cover provided by snowstorm to rout 40,000 Russians with 8,000 Swedes under the command of skilled and professional generals.

What followed was one of the great reversals of modern history. The initiative passed from Sweden to Russia as Peter conquered the Baltic provinces of Livonia, Estonia, Karelia and Ingria, setting up in the process a new capital at St Petersburg and a naval base at Kronstadt, both where the River Neva meets the Gulf of Finland. Then, in 1709, Peter virtually destroyed the Swedish army at Poltava, thereby exacting full revenge for his own humiliation at Narva. How was this possible?

One reason was the different lessons drawn from Narva by the two protagonists, which indicated a striking contrast in their characters. Peter deduced that what was needed was perseverance and a long-term policy of learning from Sweden while, at the same time, wearing her down. 'I know', he said 'the Swedes will long continue to be victorious, but in time they will teach us to beat them' (Lentin 1973: ch. 1). He therefore introduced extensive military reforms which helped transform the Russian army; these are dealt with on pp. 40–3. Charles, on the other hand, allowed victory at Narva to go to his head. He assumed that the Russians could be defeated at will and, in his contempt for Peter, he allowed himself to be diverted away from Russia between 1700 and 1708. Having wrongly identified Poland as his most dangerous enemy Charles stubbornly refused to extricate himself from the complex morass until he had achieved his objective: 'Even if I should have to remain here fifty years, I would not leave this country until Augustus is dethroned'.

Second, Peter used the respite given by Charles's campaigns in Poland to strengthen Russia's political and industrial base so that he could focus all the resources available to him on the struggle with Sweden and prepare for the inevitable climax. The methods used and the degree of success are examined in Chapter 3. Charles, by contrast, rapidly depleted Sweden's already limited resources, making no comparable effort to strengthen Sweden's infrastructure through reform. While Peter built and renewed, Charles wasted his energies in trying to sort out the complex policies of Poland. It is true that he eventually managed

Map 2   Peter the Great at war

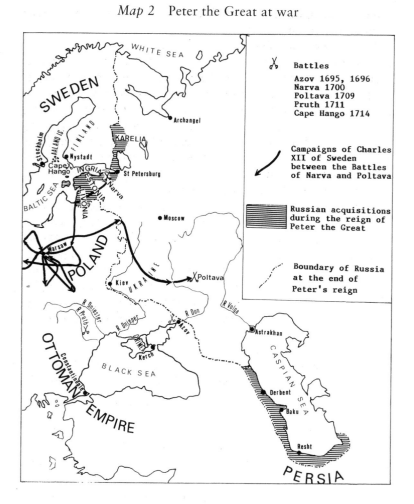

to install his own nominee, Stanislaus Leszczynski on the Polish throne but, as M. S. Anderson maintains, 'the men and money spent on these Polish struggles meant some corresponding weakening of the Swedish hold on the Baltic provinces' (Anderson 1978: ch. 4). Thus, when Charles invaded Russia in 1708, Sweden was already at the point of exhaustion. Worse, however, was to follow as Charles used up an entire army to no purpose. As a result of Charles's campaigns, the drain on the Swedish population was even greater than that later placed on

France by Napoleon, amounting to 30 per cent of the males eligible for military service.

A third factor in the Russian victory was that Peter ultimately proved the more effective military strategist, even if Charles remained the better tactician. Peter had learned from Narva to keep out of Charles's reach. Hence he withdrew before the advancing Swedes and followed a highly effective scorched-earth policy, burning crops, hiding corn stocks and concealing the livestock. The Swedes were thus unable to live off the land. The problem was made worse because Charles XII's supply army, led by Lewenhaupt, was cut off and defeated. At the same time Peter harried the Swedes, losing brief skirmishes at Holowczyn, Cerkova, Opressa, but inflicting unacceptable losses on the invader. Charles, meanwhile, became increasingly frustrated at being unable to close with the Russians and display his tactical skills on the battlefield. Worse, he made a serious strategic blunder which no amount of tactical brilliance could later rectify. Instead of recapturing the Baltic, or even moving on Moscow, Charles allowed himself to be deflected deep into the Ukraine, stretching his supply lines to breaking point and ending up over 600 miles from the Baltic.

The reason Charles did this was a fourth factor in the outcome of the war. He gambled everything on the hope that the Ukraine would revolt against Russian rule and that the dissident Ukrainian commander, Mazeppa, would provide 50,000 Cossack reinforcements for the Swedes. In fact, the insurrection was contained by Peter, who made a pre-emptive strike by sending a Russian army under Menshikov against Mazeppa. Eventually, a paltry 1,300 went over to Charles, and Mazeppa, in any case, proved an unreliable ally. In the meantime Peter had conducted an active propaganda campaign designed to prevent the majority of the Cossacks from joining the Swedes, accusing the latter of being heretics who 'deny the doctrines of the true religion and spit on the picture of the Blessed Virgin' (Durant 1963: ch. 12). He had also sown doubts about Mazeppa's greed and propagated the belief that Mazeppa was aiming not to liberate the whole of the Ukraine but to return it to Polish sovereignty. And to leave the Cossacks in no doubt about the serious consequences of any general revolt, he sent a detachment to destroy Mazeppa's capital and kill its inhabitants.

21

A fifth factor was the Russian climate, which benefited Peter against the Swedes, as it was later to assist Alexander I against Napoleon, and Stalin against Hitler. Any winter campaign on the great plains of eastern Europe presents colossal difficulties for an invader, but the winter of 1708–9 was probably the worst in four centuries. According to W. Durant's evocative description:

> It was especially severe everywhere in Europe: the Baltic froze so deeply that heavily laden wagons crossed the Sound on ice; in Germany the fruit trees died; in France the Rhône, in Venice the canals, were covered with ice. In the Ukraine snow blanketed the ground from October 1 to April 5; birds fell dead in their flight; saliva congealed in its passage from the mouth to the ground; wine and spirits froze into solid blocks; firewood would not burn in the open air; and the wind cut like a knife over the level plains and into the face.
>
> (Durant 1963: ch. 12)

An eyewitness to the sufferings of the Swedish army wrote:

> You could see some without hands, some without feet, some without ears or noses, many creeping along in the manner of quadrupeds.

This was confirmed by a Swedish officer:

> . . . the cold was beyond description, some hundred men of the regiment being injured by the freezing away of their private parts or by loss of feet, hands, noses. . . . With my own eyes, I beheld dragoons and cavalrymen sitting upon their horses stone-dead with their reins in their hands in so tight a grip that they could not be loosened until the fingers were cut off.
>
> (Massie 1981: ch. 35)

As a direct result of these winter privations, and the losses in skirmishes with the Russians, the Swedish army had shrunk by the spring of 1709 from 44,000 to 24,000. One of the Swedes, Count Piper, wrote that 'The army is in an indescribably pitiful state' (Massie 1981: ch. 35). But Charles rejected all advice to withdraw, still utterly convinced that he could recreate the scenario of Narva. 'I and the army are in very good condition. The enemy has been beaten and put to flight in all the engagements' (Massie 1981: ch. 35).

22

Peter's assessment was very different. He considered that the Swedes were now sufficiently weakened for the Russians to risk a direct engagement. When they laid siege to Poltava in the summer of 1709, therefore, the Swedes found themselves confronted by 42,000 Russians. Charles's plan was a surprise attack, but he lacked the technical means of carrying this through. Peter had learned from the Swedes the importance of an overwhelming preponderance of artillery; it has been estimated that the Russian cannon fired five times as many rounds during the Battle of Poltava as the Swedish. In addition, the Swedish musketeers ran out of ammunition, which meant that the Russian infantry were able to destroy them. Of the 19,000 Swedes who joined battle, nearly 7,000 were killed or wounded and 2,760 were taken prisoner. Poltava was therefore an unqualified triumph for the Russians. According to Massie, 'In its casualty figures as well as its outcome, it was a reversal of every previous battle between Peter and Charles'.

Poltava proved the turning point of the Great Northern War. Sweden was in total disarray, her king cut off in self-imposed exile in Turkey until 1724, and her expenditure exceeding her revenues threefold. Although Peter himself came close to the edge of disaster at the Pruth in 1711 (see p. 26), he recovered his nerve and a proper sense of priorities, proceeding to mop up the remainder of the Swedish Empire in the eastern Baltic. Russian troops overran Finland between 1713 and 1714. Peter also became more heavily involved in European diplomacy after 1713 although, as discussed on p. 35, with mixed success. He even extended Russian interest to Poland, helping remove Stanislaus Leszczynski and restore his long-time ally, Augustus.

But Peter's main achievement in the decade after Poltava was to destroy Sweden's maritime power and install Russian naval supremacy in the Baltic. The preparation and measures, dealt with on p. 43, bore fruit at the Battle of Cape Hango in 1714 in which the Russian fleet achieved a stunning victory over the Swedes. The main reason for this success was Peter's use of a large number of galleys which were able to outmanoeuvre the larger Swedish warships which had become becalmed after a sudden change in the weather. Peter had shown considerable foresight in introducing to the Baltic a type of vessel which had previously been confined to the Mediterranean: it was of shallower draught than the more conventional ship of the line and was not dependent on the wind. It therefore had a considerable advantage in the enclosed waters of the Baltic, and was highly successful operating just off the coast or between islands. The Swedes had no immediate answer and could not prevent Russia from taking over the Aaland Islands and raiding the Swedish mainland. At one point Stockholm itself was threatened.

The Great Northern War dragged on until 1721, longer than Peter wanted and Sweden could afford. The terms of the Treaty of Nystadt, however, acknowledged that the balance of power in the Baltic had been changed irrevocably. Sweden ceded to Russia her former provinces of Ingria, Estonia, Livonia and Karelia. Most of Finland and the Aaland Islands were restored. Although this may seem a major concession, Peter was aware that to insist on retaining these would probably have prolonged the war well into its third decade and that Russian resources would have been hard-pressed to guarantee their defence in the future. The Treaty of Nystadt showed considerable Russian restraint. Peter took only those territories which were essential to his policies of modernization and westernization and which could be integrated properly into the Russian Empire. He also wished to avoid having to fight a war with a vengeful Sweden within the next ten years or so. For this reason he also undertook not to interfere in Sweden's domestic affairs, especially the succession. When, therefore, he celebrated Nystadt with characteristic personal excess, Peter was confident that he had a last achieved his major objective.

The conflict with the Ottoman Empire

Although conflicts between Turkey and Russia preceded the reign of Peter the Great, they had usually been within the context of a crusade, Russia having joined with other powers such as Austria, Venice and the papacy in a more general offensive. Peter, however, thought in more specific terms. His aim was to break through the Crimea and establish a port and naval base on the Black Sea as a counterpart to those he proposed to construct on the Baltic. In addition to a window on to the west, therefore, Russia would open one on to the south and the Mediterranean. In the process, Peter intended to subject the Crimean Tartars, thereby making up for Golitsyn's unsuccessful campaigns of 1677 and 1689. In practice, Peter's policies towards Turkey met with short-term success but long-term failure, the reverse of his experiences with Sweden.

Peter's first target was the Turkish port of Azov, situated at the mouth of the River Don. His initial attempt to capture it failed in 1695, largely because he was unable to prevent Turkish sea-borne forces sailing up the Don to lift the Russian siege. Peter learned from this experience that he needed greater expertise. He therefore called in from Austria and Brandenburg experts in siege warfare and constructed a series of shipyards at Voronezh which, within five months, built a fleet of 29 galleys and 1,300 barges. Equipped with these, Peter launched a second and more successful attack on Azov in 1696. The whole campaign was better prepared; the Voronezh fleet was reinforced by ships brought overland in sections from Archangel and re-assembled on the Don. This time Azov was cut off from the sea – and relief from the Turks – and had no option but to surrender after a siege lasting two months. Peter now had the prospect of consolidating Russian control on the Crimea and could, if he wished, take advantage of Turkey's diplomatic isolation and of the preoccupation of the powers of western and central Europe with the issue of the Spanish Succession.

Yet this was precisely the moment Peter chose to switch his attention to the north. He made peace with Turkey in 1699 by the Treaty of Carlowitz which left Russia in possession of Azov, although the fortresses in Russian hands on the lower Dniester were to be destroyed and the sites they occupied were to be returned to the Sultan. Peter had three reasons for pulling out with his work only half completed. One was that he had insufficient resources at this stage to go on to conquer the Crimean Peninsula and take Kerch, which was the minimum needed to ensure undisputed access to the Black Sea. Second, his Great Embassy to the West in 1697 had failed to produce a single ally against Turkey, whereas there was a definite prospect of a coalition in the north. And third, he felt that the time was right for a swift victory against Sweden. From 1699 onwards his main priority was to extend Russian control along the eastern coastline of the Baltic and he was prepared to postpone any further advances in the south in order to do this.

Peace was maintained between Russia and Turkey from 1700 to 1709. There were, however, irritants during this period.

Turkey was especially concerned about the growing Russian fleet; in 1702, therefore, the Sultan demanded the restriction of building at Voronezh and in 1703 a fortress was constructed in the Straits of Kerch to restrict Russian naval access to the Black Sea. Peter also had to agree to a frontier adjustment in Turkey's favour between 1704 and 1705. He had little choice, as he had at all costs to prevent Turkey from joining Sweden in an anti-Russian alliance. In fact, the guarantee of further peace in the south enabled Peter to give his entire attention to the Swedish invasion and win the Battle of Poltava in 1709.

Full-scale conflict broke out again in 1710. The catalyst was the Swedish king, Charles XII, in exile in Turkey after his defeat at Poltava. He did what he could to persuade the Sultan, Ahmed III, to take up arms against Russia and to assist his own passage through Poland so that he could resume the struggle against Peter from the north. The Sultan had his own reasons for hostility against Russia: he accused Peter of having persistently broken the treaty of 1699 by strengthening the Russian fleet at Azov. Although he preferred not to be dragged into a new conflict so soon after his life-or-death struggle with Sweden, Peter nevertheless recognized that this time war was inevitable and therefore made preparations. In particular, he negotiated with the Christian subject-peoples living within the Balkan provinces of the Ottoman Empire, especially the Moldavians, Wallachians, Bulgarians and Greeks. In 1711 he issued two proclamations inciting them to rise against Turkish rule – and then sent a Russian army across the Danube to support them.

The result was disastrous. The Russians were surrounded on the Pruth by a much larger Turkish force and were resoundingly defeated in a battle which lasted nearly two days. Peter himself faced the possibility of going into captivity and could even have suffered the ultimate humiliation of being exhibited in Constantinople in a cage. In desperation, he instructed his envoy to the Grand Vizier, who commanded the Turks, to agree to any terms 'apart from slavery'. He was even willing, should the demand be made, to give up Livonia, Estonia and Karelia – everything except St Petersburg. As a sweetener he proposed a personal gift of 150,000 roubles to the Grand Vizier. While he awaited the Turkish response it must also have crossed his mind that Charles XII would be hastening to the scene of the battle to urge the Grand Vizier to impose the most stringent terms possible.

Why had Peter sunk to such depths so soon after the peak of his success at Poltava? Perhaps the main reason is that he behaved in a way which was completely out of character. Throwing aside his usual caution, he attempted a bold stroke to achieve a swift resolution but succeeded only in becoming hopelessly entangled. There is, in fact, a great deal in common between Charles XII's invasion of Russia and Peter's attack across the Dniester. Both were hastily improvised at the last minute; both trusted to unreliable allies which failed in the event to deliver sufficient support – just as Charles was let down by the Ukrainian Cossacks, so Peter found that the only Balkan Christians who actually revolted against the Turks were those in Montenegro and Herzegovina, areas which were too distant to have any bearing at all on what happened on the Pruth. Peter, like Charles, discovered that dependence on the support of dissidents was inherently risky: they were unlikely to rebel unless the invasion occurred first, but the launching of an invasion did not guarantee an uprising. It was therefore essential to have other contingencies and a coherent overall plan.

This is precisely what Peter's campaign lacked. Like Charles, he failed to make proper provision for back-up facilities; and he moved ahead too swiftly for his supply columns to maintain effective contact. Like Charles, he was drawn into these errors by a gross underestimate of the opponent's military strength and of their ability to fight on home ground. This was due partly to arrogance born of victory: just as Charles drew the wrong conclusions from Narva, so Peter derived from Poltava excessive confidence in his own invincibility. Peter also had unreliable intelligence services, which helps to explain why 38,000 Russians walked into encirclement by 200,000 Turks.

The outcome was one of the best examples in modern history of good fortune, or sheer luck. Peter's envoy returned with the terms drawn up by the Grand Vizier. The Russians were to surrender Azov, Taganrov and any remaining fortress on the Dnieper. Peter was also to refrain from any further interference in Poland and to allow Charles to return to Sweden. Nothing was said about an indemnity to Turkey or about the return of the Baltic territories to Sweden. Amazed by the moderation shown in these terms, Peter accepted with alacrity. In retrospect it may appear that the Turks lost a unique opportunity to exploit the helplessness of their main rival, a point made very forcibly by Charles XII to the Grand Vizier when he arrived at the Turkish encampment. There was, however, an underlying logic in the settlement. The Ottoman Empire had no territorial ambitions to the north other than to regain what had been lost in 1696. Neither the Sultan nor the Grand Vizier wanted to prolong the conflict with Russia or stir up resentment for the future, especially since the situation in the Crimea was inherently unstable and the support of the Crimean Tartars could not be guaranteed. As for not having twisted the knife over the Baltic territories: why should the Grand Vizier get back distant provinces, in which Turkey had no interest, for a king who had long since outstayed his welcome? And, given Turkey's desire for peace with Russia, what would have been the sense in forming an alliance with Sweden?

The keynote of Peter's future policy towards the Turks was caution. He acknowledged that 'They had the bird in their hand there, but it will not happen again' (Massie 1981: ch. 42). All the same, he bitterly regretted the loss of Azov, and with it his chance of gaining access to the Black Sea. He considered that God had turned him, like Adam, out of paradise. There was no prospect of a return during his reign. It took almost three quarters of a century for Russia to accomplish the same degree of penetration into Turkey that Peter had made into Sweden. The key settlements which gave Russia control over the north coast of the Black Sea, Kutchuk Kainardji and Jassy, were not drawn up until 1774 and 1791.

Why was Peter so unsuccessful in his efforts against Turkey in comparison with his achievements against Sweden? The reasons for the failure of the Pruth campaign have already been provided. A more general factor, however, is the difference in the size of the two countries. Turkey contained some twenty-five million people, distributed between three continents, whereas Sweden has less than one million. This meant that Turkey had a much greater military base; at no time, for example, could Sweden hope to put into the field the 200,000 troops that the Grand Vizier commanded at the Pruth. Second, the Turkish hold on the Black Sea was much stronger than that of the Swedes on the Baltic. A look at the map on p. 20 shows that Peter's acquisition of Azov was only a first step towards entry into the Black Sea. The Turks still controlled the vital Straits of Kerch; and even if the Russians had managed to capture these, access to the

Mediterranean could have been achieved only by capturing the Bosphorus and the Dardanelles, which ran through the very heart of the Ottoman Empire. Securing a Russian outlet in the Baltic was geographically less complex; Sweden had only one stranglehold – the Gulf of Finland – to Turkey's three.

Third, the Ottoman Empire was far more adept than Sweden at defending itself. Although in decline, it still had a strong sense of survival which precluded campaigns deep into enemy territory with inadequate supply lines. Sweden was defeated because she overextended herself. Finally, from 1699, Peter chose to focus his attention on Sweden. He did not have sufficient resources to take on Turkey as well. Had he chosen the latter he might have made greater inroads into the Black Sea. But this would have meant no new capital on the Baltic and no window on to the west. Catherine the Great was able to push back the Turkish frontiers in the south only because Peter's first objective, access to the Baltic, had already been secured.

Russian expansion in Asia during Peter's reign

Most attention is given by historians to Russia's expansion westwards and southwards. But there is another dimension in Russian history – the movement of her frontier eastwards. This had normally, and especially in the seventeenth century, been the principal manifestation of Russia's territorial growth. Peter's intentions were to extend the already vast expanse of Siberia, to improve relations with China, to dominate the trade routes to India, and to strengthen Russia's position in relation to Persia in the region of the Caspian Sea. All of these were in his mind throughout the reign, but were given lower priority than the struggles with Sweden and Turkey. This meant that Peter's activity in Asia began in earnest only after 1714, reaching its peak after the Baltic issues had been finally settled in 1721 by the Treaty of Nystadt. By the time of his death in 1725 Peter's achievements in Asia had been significant but hardly spectacular.

The Russian Empire had reached the Pacific long before the period covered by this book. In what little time he found to devote to Siberia, Peter considered the possibilities of opening up new tracts of land, of extending Siberia to the remotest parts and perhaps even into the American continent. Hence he showed interest in the Sea of Okhotsk, captured the Kurile Islands and authorized the annexation of the remote Kamchatka Peninsula which, in terms of area, was the largest territorial acquisition of the reign. He also commissioned a Danish captain in his service, Vitus Bering, to investigate the possibility of a land bridge connecting Siberia and North America and spent some of his final hours drawing up detailed instructions. Bering shortly afterwards gave his name – and his life – to the 53-mile strait between the two continents and his detailed cartography opened up the entire coastline of Alaska to Russian trade and settlement. Peter deserves much of the credit for this development and can hardly be blamed for Alexander II's decision a century and a half later to sell Alaska to the United States for $7 million. Less successful were Peter's efforts to exploit the reputed mineral wealth of Siberia; several expeditions all failed in their search for gold.

Contacts with China were an inevitable result of Russian expansion eastwards. Peter was attracted by the prospects of regular trade with Cathay and took the initiative in sending embassies to Peking, the first as far back as 1692, the second in 1719. These met with a punctilious but aloof reception from the Manchu Emperor K'ang-hsi, who was committed to a policy of economic and diplomatic isolation as a means of preserving China's ancient heritage. Peter therefore found that his policy of opening windows was unwelcome, incurring a rebuff from the Chinese. In the final years of Peter's reign the volume of trade between Russia and China actually diminished and he frankly acknowledged his failure here.

He was always more hopeful of bringing under Russian control the overland trading route with India, which extended through the Khyber Pass and across the steppes of Central Asia. The middle section of this journey was on occasion imperilled by two rival rulers, the Khans of Khiva and Bokhara. Peter set himself the apparently modest objective of bringing these under his sovereignty, or at least under Russian protection. He failed on both counts. An expedition despatched in 1716 was destroyed the following year and its unfortunate leader, Cherassky, was beheaded, stuffed and displayed in the courtyard of the Khan's palace. Peter might have mounted punitive expeditions to deal with incidents like this but preferred instead to concentrate his resources on a fourth area.

This was the Persian Empire, which, under the Safavid dynasty, was in the process of irreversible decline. Peter hoped to bring it under Russian diplomatic and commercial influence, in the process controlling the silk trade with India and replacing the existing route via Turkey to the Mediterranean. The Shah, understandably, was not fully co-operative and Peter decided to resort to more direct measures. He proposed to take advantage of Persia's internal weakness and establish a permanent Russian presence along the western and southern shores of the Caspian Sea, as well as in the Caucasus. In the short term he succeeded. In 1722 Peter led a combined naval and military expedition down the Volga to Astrakhan, then along the west coast of the Caspian Sea to Derbent. After a second campaign, in which the Russians captured Baku and Resht in 1723, the Shah had no option but to cede to Peter all his provinces bordering on the Caspian Sea. Peter also managed to avoid a new war with Turkey, which had become seriously alarmed at the prospect of further Russian penetration into the Caucasus. As a result of French mediation in 1724, Persia's Caucasian possessions were divided by the Treaty of Constantinople into Russian and Turkish spheres of influence.

In the longer term, however, all of Peter's gains in the area were cancelled out. M. S. Anderson goes so far as to say that eventually 'his Persian war proved an expensive failure' (1978: ch. 6). As Massie points out, some of the Caspian Sea provinces were returned to Persia by Anna in 1732, who found the cost of maintaining a permanent Russian presence in them prohibitive. Nor was it possible at this stage to extend Russian rule into the area supposedly under Russian influence in the Caucasus. Overall, Peter had done little more than set up a marker for the future; it remained for Catherine the Great to bring Armenia and Georgia within the Russian Empire.

Russian diplomacy and the great powers

Peter was more successful as a warrior than as a diplomat. There was no tradition of Russian diplomacy behind him and during the first part of the Great Northern War he engaged little interest and support from the west. After his military success at Poltava in 1709 the powers took him more seriously. Their reactions were, however, mixed and they alternated between courting and trying to contain Russia. Peter reacted to this cautiously but, on the whole, without finesse. He seemed to be unfamiliar and uncomfortable with his new diplomatic role. Russia's successful involvement in the mainstream of European diplomacy lay very much in the future.

Peter lacked the sort of diplomatic tradition and experience which existed in the foreign ministries of all the major European powers and many of the minor states as well. This was all too obvious in the early part of his reign when he had to work particularly hard at trying to interest the western states in the possibility of an alliance with Russia. One of the major purposes of the Great Embassy of 1697 was to win western diplomatic support for Russian expansion into the Black Sea and the Baltic. In this he was generally unsuccessful. He failed, for example, to secure an alliance with the Holy Roman Emperor against Turkey. England and the Dutch Republic made it clear that they did not wish to be drawn in, while the Spanish Succession issue kept Austria preoccupied. Hence, according to Anderson, 'The whole configuration of international relations was, at least for the time being, unfavourable to Peter's hopes' (1978: ch. 3). He had to be satisfied with a more limited northern coalition comprising Denmark and Augustus II of Saxony and Poland.

As the War of the Spanish Succession gradually took its toll on resources, the combatants on both sides sought to draw in the states involved in the Great Northern War which was being fought at the same time. British diplomats tried in 1700 and 1702 to mediate to bring to an end the war between Russia and Sweden. Although these attempts failed, Britain went some way to keeping Sweden amenable, guaranteeing to support her against Denmark over access through the Sound, and sending the Duke of Marlborough in 1707 to try to persuade Charles XII to throw in his lot with the Grand Alliance against France. In all this the target and focus of Britain's attention was Sweden, not Russia; much more credence was given to Sweden's military strength, especially after Charles XII's spectacular victory at Narva in 1700. Britain also hoped to release Saxony and Poland from the Northern War, considering even these to be more valuable than Russia as potential allies. France was less inclined to dismiss Russia outright, hoping that Peter might be persuaded to invade Transylvania and stir up nationalist problems with the Austrian dominions. On the other hand, this was very much a peripheral role envisaged for Russia, and France did not push it very far. She was anxious to avoid antagonizing Sweden which, like Britain, she regarded as the more formidable power. The Russian victory at Poltava changed the whole perception that the western powers had of Russia. A German observer stated at the time:

> You can imagine how the great revolution in the north has astounded many people. It is commonly being said that the Tsar will be formidable to the whole of Europe, that he will be as though a 'Turk of the North'.
>
> (Rady 1990: ch. 6)

Reactions to this change were sometimes positive, but frequently hostile.

For a while, especially between 1709 and 1711, Russia was more actively sought by the powers as a possible mediator. Both Britain and France now considered that Russia might help bring to an end the War of the Spanish Succession. Louis XIV was particularly desperate for peace after a series of military defeats and the disastrous famines experienced by France in 1709 and 1710. Alternatively, Russia was now seen as a potential ally. The French realized that she would be valuable as a threat both to British naval power in the Baltic and to the military strength of Austria in central Europe. From the British perspective, Russia could be a useful member of the Grand Alliance against France. Peter's response to both sides was characteristically cautious, since his main priorities were to secure a successful outcome to the Great Northern War and to clear up the debris created by his unsuccessful campaign against Turkey in 1711.

Once the War of the Spanish Succession had been ended in 1713, there was no longer a need to secure Russia as an ally. Instead, Russia came to be perceived as a threat, on two counts. First, Peter's treaty with Mecklenburg-Schwerin, allowing Russia the use of military and naval facilities, aroused fears in Denmark and Austria that Sweden's withdrawal from Germany was about to be replaced by Russian penetration. Russia was also seen by Britain as a long-term threat to Hanover, with which the accession of George I in 1714 had brought dynastic union. The pressure on Peter from these various sources became

Map 3 Europe at war during the reign of Peter the Great

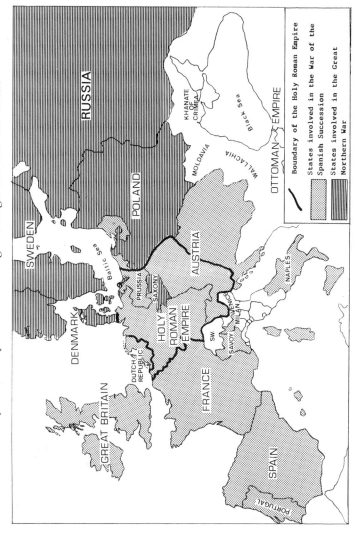

Boundary of the Holy Roman Empire

States involved in the War of the
Spanish Succession

States involved in the Great
Northern War

so strong that he reluctantly decided to pull out of Mecklenburg in 1717. Meanwhile, Britain was even more concerned about Russia's threat to British naval power and the possibility that she might monopolize the trade in naval stores in the Baltic. Increasingly, therefore, Russia became the target of British diplomacy and statesmen like Stanhope tried to salvage as much as possible of the ruined Swedish Empire to counter the rise of Russia. In 1720, for example, an Anglo-Swedish alliance was signed and the British navy prevented any large-scale Russian operations against the Swedish coast.

Peter thus aroused a greater reaction from the rest of Europe than had any of his predecessors. In this context, Peter was sufficiently aware of his increased importance to proclaim himself Emperor – as well as Tsar – in 1721. But this could not hide the fact that Peter was uncomfortable with a diplomatic role and was outclassed by the likes of Stanhope, Cardinal Fleury, Cardinal Alberoni and Elizabeth Farnese. He had three successes, but all were limited. First, by 1725, there were over twenty-one Russian embassies in Europe, compared with one at the beginning of the reign. Much, however, remained to be done to develop their expertise when dealing with more experienced officials in western Europe. Second, Peter arranged a number of dynastic unions which linked Russia more closely with other European states. On the other hand, all of these involved minor German states like Courland, Brunswick-Wolfenbuttel and Mecklenburg-Schwerin; as yet there were no connections with Europe's major dynasties. Third, Peter was able for the first time to project Russia as a desirable ally. When he visited Paris in 1717 he argued:

> France has lost its allies in Germany; Sweden, almost destroyed, cannot be of any help to it; the power of the Emperor has grown infinitely; and I, the Tsar, come to offer myself to France to replace Sweden . . . put me in the place of Sweden.
> (Anderson 1978: ch. 4)

Again, he did not really achieve what he wanted. Although Cardinal Fleury agreed in 1717 to draw up the Treaty of Amsterdam between France, Russia and Prussia, he made it clear that it should carry no military obligations and that it was of secondary importance to the Triple Alliance between Britain, France and the Dutch Republic.

Despite a generally mediocre performance in diplomacy, Peter did show three important attributes. One was a degree of caution which his contemporaries sometimes found exasperating. He did not throw away his military victories by trying to extend Russia's commitments through diplomacy, a mistake which had frequently been made by Louis XIV. The second was an instinctive awareness of when he was on tenuous ground. When he was particularly hard-pressed he withdrew before being confronted by a major crisis, as was the case in Mecklenburg-Schwerin. Finally, he also knew when it was essential to take a firm stance and back diplomacy by a show of military power. For example, he backed Russian demands at the Nystadt conference by his threat to deploy 115,000 regular soldiers, 25,000 of whom were immediately available in Finland and 40,000 transportable by galley for an attack on Sweden. Peter was in his element when he had the opportunity to use the threat of force as a lever for diplomacy and, on this occasion at least, nullified all the efforts deployed by Britain on behalf of Sweden.

St Petersburg was eventually to join London, Paris and Vienna as one of the diplomatic centres of Europe – but not under Peter the Great. The real foundations for Russian diplomatic success in the eighteenth century were to be laid by two foreign ministers, Ostermann and Bestuzhev, who spanned much of the period between 1725 and 1762. The benefit was reaped by Panin, head of the department of foreign affairs under Catherine the Great (1762–96), who was herself renowned for her combination of subtlety and ruthlessness. It could, of course, be argued that this was only possible because of the military infrastructure already established by Peter, as a result partly of the territorial expansion, covered in this chapter, and partly of the internal reforms to which we now turn.

Plate 1   Portrait of Peter the Great by Sir Godfrey Kneller,
1698. (Reproduced by permission of the Royal Collection,
Kensington Palace, London, © 1992 Her Majesty the Queen.)

Plate 2 Engraving of Peter the Great by W. Faithorne, 1698.
(© British Museum, London.)

Plate 3 Portrait of Peter the Great, Russian school, first half of the eighteenth century. (Rijksmuseum, Amsterdam.)

Plate 4   Bronze bust of Peter the Great by Carlo Rastrelli, 1723–9. (Hermitage Museum/Aurora Publishers, St Petersburg.)

Plate 5   Portrait of Peter the Great by Carl Moor, 1717.
(Courtesy of the Mansell Collection.)

Plate 6 Wax figure made in 1725 after Rastrelli's bust. (Hermitage Museum/Aurora Publishers, St Petersburg.)

Plate 7   Peter the Great founding St Petersburg. Gravure after
A. V. Kotzebue. (Courtesy of the Mansell Collection.)

Plate 8 *Peter the Great and the building of St Petersburg* by V. Serov, 1907. (Tetryakov Gallery, Moscow.)

3
Peter the Great's internal reforms

An introductory analysis and historiography

In any analysis of Peter the Great's internal reforms two themes are generally highlighted: their motivation and their impact. Over the former there is a general consensus, while the latter has attracted a considerable range of views.

Most historians consider that there was a powerful stimulus behind almost all the changes made during Peter's reign: the demands imposed on Russian resources by the Great Northern War. Lentin, for example, argues that 'The changes wrought by Peter between 1700 and 1709 stemmed . . . from the immediate exigencies of war' (1973: ch. 2). Anderson agrees: 'war and the demands it generated were the mainspring of much of Peter's innovating and creative activity in Russia' (1978: ch. 5). E. N. Williams maintains that reacting to the military situation was 'the raison d'être of all other reforms' (1970: ch. 10). The same line is taken by Yaney, Massie, Sumner and Raeff.

War also dictated the style and pace of reform. Dukes, for one, believes that 'Peter's reforms in government as elsewhere were improvised rather than carefully planned, particularly in the beginning' (1974: ch. 5). Massie goes further, making an important distinction, in the pace of the reforms, between the periods before and after Poltava. Initial changes were introduced rapidly and with a minimum of preliminary research and preparation while later in the reign there was more time to rationalize the whole structure. At no stage, however, did Peter have an overall design or blueprint; he was guided largely by necessity, and found the answer in transplanting ideas from the West. When Peter said, after his humiliation at Narva, that Russia would learn from the Swedes how eventually to defeat them, he was expressing his underlying attitude to change.

There is much greater disagreement over the effects of the reforms than over their motivation. Were they, for example, revolutionary – a complete break with the Muscovite past? Or were they merely a continuation of changes already set in motion by Peter's predecessors? Within this structural contrast there are also different shades of emphasis. If the change was revolutionary, was this beneficial or destructive to Russia's interests? If it was evolutionary did it signify genuine progress or was it obstructive to genuine and urgently needed reform?

Peter was first given the credit for being revolutionary in the positive sense by a group of Russian intellectuals known as the 'Westernizers'. Several nineteenth-century historians eulogized Peter as a transformer. Chaadeyev, for example, argued that Peter the Great saw Russia as 'only a blank sheet of paper. With his powerful hand he wrote on it "Europe and the West"' (Rady 1990: ch. 5). Soloviev, too, maintained that 'No people have ever equalled the heroic feat performed by the Russians during the first quarter of the eighteenth century' (Raeff 1963: p. 82). Of the twentieth-century historians, the one most inclined to see Peter in this light is Marc Raeff, according to whom Peter brought about one of the five great revolutions experienced by Russia since the Middle Ages. As a result of each,

> the Russians felt that they had not only undergone institutional changes but that, as a people, they had been transformed spiritually, culturally, psychologically.
>
> (Raeff 1963: Introduction)

Furthermore,

> Whatever their roots in the past of Muscovy, the reforms of Peter the Great marked the beginning of a new era in Russia's public life. It is hardly a exaggeration to speak of Peter the Great as the founder of the modern Russian state who set the

framework of its institutional development for the entire course of the eighteenth and nineteenth centuries.

A negative view of Peter the revolutionary was introduced during the nineteenth century by the 'Slavophiles' who challenged the view of the Westernizers that Peter's changes had been to the benefit of Russia; instead, Peter had permanently damaged the very fabric of traditional society by introducing alien ideas and institutions. The strongest critic of Peter in the twentieth century has been Berdyaev, who drew a direct parallel between Peter and the destructive impact of Lenin. The Petrine and Bolshevik Revolutions, he said, showed:

> the same barbarity, violence, forcible application of certain principles from above downwards, the same rupture of organic development and repudiation of tradition ... the same desire sharply and radically to change the type of civilization.
>
> (N. Berdyaev, *The Origin of Russian Communism*, Introduction)

There have, however, always been those prepared to deny that Peter the Great was in any sense a revolutionary. S. F. Platonov asked in 1904:

> Was his activity traditional, or did it represent a sharp and sudden revolution in the life of the Muscovite state, for which the country was entirely unprepared? The answer is quite clear. Peter's reforms were not a revolution, either in their substance or their results. Peter was not a 'Royal revolutionary', as he is sometimes called.
>
> (Raeff 1963: p. 88)

There was not sharp break in political or economic or social development, maintained Platonov, and Peter could not be considered the originator of any 'cultural trend'. If anything, he merely accelerated previous processes – a necessary but not particularly exceptional contribution to Russian development. A more negative angle is provided by the nineteenth-century Russian Marxist, Plekhanov. Peter's rule, according to his analysis, took on more of the characteristics of an oriental despotism, a specific form of economic and social organization recognized in Marxist thought. Peter's modernization was profoundly necessary to bring Russia into line with bourgeois

39

developments elsewhere in Europe. But it was only partially accomplished because the system held him back. All Peter managed to do, therefore, was to edge Russia a little closer to the stage of evolution which would make possible the type of revolution advocated by Marx, the overturn of the entire social and economic base.

Most historians now adopt the line that Peter introduced changes which were within the context of Muscovite developments and that he did not place his imprint on a 'blank sheet' as claimed by Chaadeyev. Three examples may be cited of this approach. According to Anderson, 'Russia under Peter the Great can thus be regarded as undergoing, in the main, a process of forced and greatly accelerated evolution rather than of true revolution'. On the other hand, Anderson concedes, the pace of his changes must have appeared revolutionary at the time. This confirms the view of Lentin that Peter's role was

> that of a catalyst, speeding up policies already slowly under way. However, he acted with such vigour and energy that his actions certainly seemed revolutionary to those who were subjected to them. . . . It was, then, the pace, volume and external aspects of reform that were revolutionary.
>
> (Lentin 1973: ch. 4)

Somewhat earlier, Sumner had provided another but complementary perspective. Although conceding that most of Peter's changes depended on previous developments he nevertheless identified four specific changes which were radical in that they had no roots in past developments; these were 'the education of Russians abroad, the abolition of the Patriarchate, the creation of the navy, and the making of a new capital, St Petersburg'.

The ideas outlined in this preliminary survey will be developed, as appropriate, in the following sections which cover the specific areas of Peter's internal policies.

The army

The Russian defeat at Narva came as a profound shock: there had been nothing comparable since the defeat of the Swedes by Brandenburg at Fehrbellin in 1675. An official report, written by Ivan Pososhkov, pulled no punches:

40

The infantry are armed with bad muskets and do not know how to use them. They fight with their sidearms, with lances, and halberds and even these are blunt. For every foreigner killed there are three, four, and even more Russians killed. As for our cavalry, we are ashamed to look at them ourselves, let alone show them to the foreigner. They consist of sickly, ancient horses, blunt sabres, puny, badly dressed men who do not know how to wield their weapons.

(Massie 1981: ch. 26)

The reasons for this humiliation have already been explained on pp. 18–19. Peter met the emergency by introducing changes at all levels of the armed forces. He began by disbanding the Streltsy and making the Guards the new nucleus. Numbers were increased by the application of more systematic conscription based from 1705 onwards on a series of general levies. By the early 1720s these had produced a standing army of 200,000 regulars which could be supplemented by 100,000 Cossacks and other auxiliaries. Training was overhauled by the introduction of new manuals. The emphasis was very much on discipline in action, including the co-ordinated fire of platoons and the more regular use by cavalry units of charges, wheeling and regrouping. He also introduced a simple and functional uniform of green broadcloth and three-cornered hats. Weapons were gradually replaced by the most modern available. While in England Peter had purchased up to 40,000 flintlocks with ring bayonets. These were imitated in Russia, 30,000 a year being manufactured by 1706. Peter also gave a much-needed impetus to the development of Russian artillery, the metal at first being provided by the melting down of a least of a quarter of Russia's church bells. Within a year of Narva Russia was already outproducing Sweden and was also learning from the latter the need for light, manoeuvrable, and standardized pieces. By the time of Poltava the Russians had an unassailable lead here.

How revolutionary were these reforms? Extensive though they were, they were not entirely without precedent. Dukes, for instance, argues that the army was developed during Peter's time on a foundation which he himself attributed to his father Alexis, and which may more accurately be placed in the reign of his grandfather Michael (1974: ch. 4). There had, for example, already been instances of large-scale recruitment

41

during 1654–67 for the struggle against Poland. Peter's predecessors had also been influenced by western ideas and practice. The *novogo stroya*, or 'new formation' directly imitated German methods and was led by German officers; this is seen by Anderson as an early example of 'a massive irruption of foreign influences into Russian military life' (1978: ch. 5), providing a strong base for Peter's military reforms so that 'in military affairs, as in so many other areas, he accelerated and intensified a process of change which had begun long before he was born' (1978: ch. 5). Even the idea of using western training methods was not original; the existing infantry manuals, dating from 1647, had been based on a German manual of 1615.

It could also be argued that Peter's military reforms were by no means uniformly effective. Against the Turks, for example, Peter met in 1711 with the sort of military failure which would have been familiar to his seventeenth-century predecessors. There were also innate problems throughout the army which he was unable to eradicate. At the highest level the long-standing friction and rivalry between the leading generals reached a new intensity in the relations between Sheremetev, Menshikov and Repnin. Lower down, the quality of officers remained so variable that no amount of foreign imports could guarantee consistently effective command. At the bottom, the army was, as always, vulnerable to desertion on a massive scale. If anything, this problem was exacerbated by Peter's decrees on recruitment which virtually ensured that peasant conscripts were swallowed up into the army for life.

But allowing for a certain degree of continuity in the changes to the Russian army does not alter the basic point that Peter's reforms were sweeping and fundamental. Russia could not have emerged as the victor over Sweden without them. She could only have survived, weakened and further depleted. As it was, Russia moved through the eighteenth century as one of the continent's four military powers, her troops reaching the Rhine during the War of the Austrian Succession (1740–7) and providing by far the greatest threat to Frederick the Great's Prussia during the Seven Years War (1756–63). At the end of the Napoleonic Wars the Russians were even installed in Paris. There was certainly no precedent in Russian history for this. The military changes were also directly responsible for the establishment of the new administrative structure dealt with on pp. 46–50. The army even permeated the offices *within* this structure. According to Yaney, Peter's army dominated the entire government on all its levels until the 1760s: 'Army chiefs occupied commanding positions in the central offices, army veterans staffed the civil administration, and army units intervened actively in civil affairs' (1973: ch. 1). This was, however, relatively short-lived, as Catherine the Great subsequently undertook an extensive campaign to demilitarize the civil government.

The navy

Sir Godfrey Kneller's painting (plate 1) shows Peter the Great clad in armour with the fleet he created in the background. This is one of the relatively few instances where an idealized portrait bears more than a passing resemblance to reality. Peter is usually seen as the father of the Russian navy, an achievement which was, in Anderson's view, 'a far more abrupt and self-conscious break with the past than any of the tsar's military successes' (1978: ch. 5).

There were fewer precedents here than in Peter's other reforms. Ivan the Terrible had toyed with the idea of creating a large sea-going fleet, but this had been confined to a few ships based at Archangel on the White Sea or on the internal river network. Peter showed unparalleled interest and personal commitment which extended from the beginning of his reign until the very day of his death. His first effective campaign, against Azov in 1695, followed months of intensive shipbuilding, while his major preoccupation during the Great Embassy to the West was acquainting himself with new techniques of naval construction at Zaandam and Deptford. He afforded the navy the highest priority; this is shown in the steady increase in expenditure from 81,000 roubles in 1701 to 204,000 in 1706, 700,000 in 1715 and 1.2 million in 1721. By the end of the reign the size of the fleet had grown to 800 galleys and 48 ships of the line. The infrastructure for all this was also carefully developed. Six and a quarter million roubles were spent on building the Admiralty Quay in St Petersburg and the Kronstadt naval base, while the admiralty itself became one of the largest enterprises in Europe, responsible for a huge labour force and for the exploitation and processing of naval materials like timber, cloth, cordage and pitch. Underlying these developments was an increasingly complex administrative structure based on the navy *prikaz*, or chancellery, set up in 1698, followed by the admiralty *prikaz* in 1701 and the admiralty college in 1718.

In the short term Peter's changes produced a remarkable degree of success. The navy was responsible for the only real gains against Turkey, even though these were later lost by the failure of the army. It played a complementary, but vital, role in the struggle against Sweden. Although Swedish military might was broken by the Russian army in Poltava, it was the navy which ensured the collapse of Sweden's empire in the Baltic through the victory at Cape Hango in 1714 and the capture of the Aaland Islands. The navy, in short, enabled Peter to adopt a more global strategy and to extend the range of the conflict to Finland and even the Swedish mainland. Above all, it was the success of the Russian navy that eventually pressurized Sweden into accepting the terms of the Treaty of Nystadt in 1721.

On the other hand, the achievements of Peter the Great were not sustained by his immediate successors. Anderson argues that 'since it responded to no deep national need', the Russian navy 'went into a rapid decline after the death of its creator' (1978: ch. 5). This is certainly true to the extent that Russia's access to the Baltic was now assured and, for a while, the attention of her rulers turned to Germany and Poland. In the longer term, however, the precedent established by Peter proved vital. Catherine the Great was able, in a very short time, to reactivate Russia's naval power, the motive this time being territorial expansion to create a southern coastline. What Peter had accomplished in the Baltic, Catherine eventually repeated in the Black Sea; in the process she had made the Russian fleet the second largest in the world by 1796.

Central government

Throughout his reign, Peter's personal power was absolute. This was partly a continuation of traditional Muscovite autocracy. It was, however, given a new intensity by the force of his personality and by a new theoretical base provided by Prokopovich, Procurator General of the Holy Synod. It was also upheld by the Military Regulation of 1716 which declared that the tsar is not obliged to answer to anyone in the world for his doings, but possesses power over his kingdom and land, to rule them at his will and pleasure as a Christian ruler.

(Anderson 1978: ch. 5)

But this was no justification for arbitrary rule, or tyranny, of the type which had been exercised by Ivan the Terrible in his later years. Peter strongly believed that his power should be exercised in the national interest which, in turn meant eliminating inefficiency and making maximum use of Russia's resources. According to Raeff 'Peter introduced the concept of the active, creative, goal-directed state. . . . The goal was to maximize the power of the state, which in turn was to enhance the welfare of the nation' (in Auty and Obolensky 1976: p. 123).

In order to exercise power fully, Peter needed an effective administration. This was signally lacking at the beginning of the reign. The Muscovite structure of central government comprised the *zemskii sobor*, the *duma* and the *prikazy*. These had already proved defective and were unable from the outset to meet the demands Peter placed on them. The *zemskii sobor* was an irregular institution, through which the nobility occasionally managed to exert influence on the tsar, but its history had been erratic. The *duma*, an ancient body of nobles, no longer provided effective supervision over the various departments, and its membership, had in any case, declined by over 60 per cent during the 1690s. The fifty *prikazy*, or chancelleries, had badly defined and overlapping functions which meant that the function of departments comprised both national and regional issues. The result was confusion and inefficiency.

The administration's deficiencies became glaringly obvious when pressure was placed upon it during Russia's conflict with Sweden which, of course, was consistently Peter's main preoccupation. The impact of war can be negative; it sometimes undermines a regime by destroying its military base, bleeding its economy and fragmenting its forces of law and order. This happened in Russia in 1916 and 1917. Alternatively, war sometimes acts as a catalyst for administrative reform since it increases the demand for recruits, the provision of military supplies and the organization of revenues. It became obvious to Peter immediately after Narva that military victory over Sweden could be accomplished only by an overhaul of the administrative infrastructure. This was not, however, attempted in one blow or as part of an overall blueprint. Instead, historians generally agree, the changes were initially unsystematic; they were immediate responses to the unpredictable needs of the most difficult phase of the war between 1700 and 1709. Anderson, for example, maintains that 'for many years efforts to improve the administration were partial, hasty and unconsidered, the work of a man preoccupied by other pressing tasks' (Anderson 1978: ch. 5).

There was more time to plan and rationalize during the last ten years of the reign, when the immediate crisis had passed, and the emphasis could move to the creation of a more permanent military power. At this stage the intention was to create machinery which would work over the longer term, although the driving force was still war. The historian who best expresses this change of tempo, if not a change of direction, is Peterson: 'The systematic reconstruction of the administrative system coincided chronologically with the final consolidation of the permanent regular military forces in the Russian Empire' (Peterson 1979). In doing this Peter was able to avoid repeating the mistakes of states, like Spain, who had made adjustments to the immediate demands of war without following up with longer-term changes: the price paid had been accelerating economic crisis and military decline.

The two major phases of administrative change were 1701–11 and 1718–25. The first dealt largely with piecemeal changes in local authorities since the later were primarily responsible for co-ordinating the resources and supplies for the war effort. A great step forward in centralization came in 1711 with the establishment of the Senate. It was intended as a short term expedient while Peter was campaigning on the Pruth. Hence 'We appoint the governing Senate to administer in our absence' with instructions 'to collect money as much as possible, for money is the artery of war'. After his return, however, he decided to use it as a permanent replacement for the *duma* and, through a series of royal decrees, extended its authority over local government, revenue and the judiciary. As yet, however, there was no effective subordinate system of government departments.

This was provided in 1718, with the most systematic and carefully planned of all Peter's administrative reforms. Nine new colleges were set up to replace the traditional *prikazy*. Colleges (or *Kollegiia*) were introduced for each of the following: war, admiralty, foreign affairs, state revenue, state expenditure, mines, manufacture, commerce and justice. Each college had a president, a vice-president and a decision-making board of nine other officials. The rest of the college was made up of various grades of administrative officials and assistants, whose operating procedures were all carefully defined by the General Regulation of 1720. The whole system was brought under the control of the senate in 1721, the presidents themselves becoming full members of the senate, which meant that the latter had, in effect, become a cabinet of ministers. By the end of the reign, the central administration had therefore been allocated specific functional responsibilities radiating outwards from a co-ordinating body. To ensure that the new machinery functioned properly, Peter introduced in 1721 the post of *Generalprokuror* of the Senate to preside over the college presidents in the absence of the tsar and to supervise the network of *fiskals*, or spies, who operated throughout the whole administration. Finally, the quality of personnel was improved by the introduction in 1722 of the Table of Ranks. This established three parallel hierarchies in the army and navy (to which were allocated 126 posts), the court (42 posts) and the administration (94 posts). There were to be fourteen parallel grades, with progressive promotion as a result of service and merit.

There has been some debate about the influences behind Peter's collegial system. One view is that the colleges owed very little to western influences and were a logical development of traditional Muscovite institutions. This was the approach of the nineteenth-century historian, Berendts, who argued that Peter imitated nothing. The principle of collegiality was already ingrained in Russia, especially in the *prikaz* network. Peter's colleges were therefore an updated version of the *prikazy*. Much the same point was made by recent Soviet historians like Sofronenko and Steshenko who wrote in 1973 that Peter's collegial reforms were the outcome of a long-term progression towards centralization, and that previous institutions already had collegial elements within them.

The second view is that western ideas and institutions *were* imitated but not slavishly; the traditional system was renovated and improved but by no means eradicated. Yaney maintains that 'The unplanned, spontaneous development of Peter's institutions suggests that their introduction was not simply a matter of transplanting Western institutions into Russian government' (Yaney 1973: ch. 2). Peter only utilized western models and concepts; he did not emulate them, nor did he want to. Hence, although the colleges derived some of their inspiration from Sweden, 'they did not resemble Swedish colleges in practice'.

The third – and best substantiated – argument is that Peter deliberately selected Swedish institutions as a pattern for transforming Russia's central administration, in the process effecting a radical change. According to Anderson, 'of all his reforms this is one of those in which foreign influence is the most obvious' (Anderson 1978: ch. 5). But the most thorough research into this has been carried out by the Swedish historian, Peterson. His conclusions, following an exceptionally detailed analysis, is that Peter planned a major overhaul of the Russian administration as early as 1714 and was directly behind the orders for its introduction and implementation. He was convinced that Sweden offered the best example and in 1716 sent Heinrich Fick to Stockholm to gather secretly as much information as possible about the Swedish colleges. Fick supplied Peter with a wide range of essential documents, including a considerable number of legislative acts. These enabled Peter to model his colleges on Swedish prototypes. The dependence was, according to Peterson, much greater than has hitherto been presumed.

> Not only was the framework of the administrative structure borrowed from Sweden, but the internal organization and activities of the various administrative organs were also patterned on those of their Swedish counterparts . . . there were connecting links to the comparable Swedish organs within each sector of the Russian administrative system that began to take form in 1718.
>
> (Peterson 1979)

The nine colleges in St Petersburg were almost exact replicas of the nine in Stockholm, down to their very titles.

Why did Peter select Sweden, which after all was his enemy, as the model for his most important changes? One reason is that he knew the Swedish system more intimately than any other, partly through the information provided by hundreds of Swedish prisoners of war, largely through the material systematically gathered and collated by Heinrich Fick. With knowledge came increasing respect. It soon became evident that Sweden was the best example in Europe of how to maximize limited resources to maintain an army in the field, not for years but for decades. Peter was also aware of the similarities between Sweden and Russia. Both were northern powers, with a limited economic base. Both were absolute monarchies in which the policies of the ruler played a vital part in the process of change, certainly by comparison with England and the Dutch Republic, where political change had owed more to a process of evolution. Finally, there was even a precedent for the importance of the personal imprint of the monarch. Fick produced a document entitled 'Concerning the Swedish administration after the introduction of absolutism' which showed how much the Swedish administration owed to the direct initiative of Charles XI (1660–97). It could therefore be argued that Peter the Great used the inspiration and methods of Charles XI to defeat his son, Charles XII.

How successful were Peter's reforms? Inevitably there were problems and shortcomings. The quality of personnel in the new institutions nearly always fell below Peter's expectations. He frequently had cause to chide the members of the senate for irresponsible behaviour, time-wasting or accepting bribes 'according to ancient and stupid customs'. The senate was also split by quarrels which sometimes degenerated into brawls with senators rolling about on the floor. Similar difficulties occurred in the colleges, initially staffed by men with inappropriate experience, expertise and education. Again, business was held back by factional rivalries between, for example, high-born Dolgoruky and self-made Menshikov, or by unseemly squabbles between some of the presidents and vice-presidents. Peter tried to promote greater initiative and responsibility in his officials. His efforts were, however, largely unsuccessful since the latter were frightened into inactivity by the Draconian punishments he imposed for making mistakes.

Despite these obvious deficiencies, Peter did introduce some positive changes. One was the important principle of specialization on the basis of function rather than geographical allocation. This is an essential feature of the civil service of any modern state. Similarly, the collegial system resulted in more effective fiscal administration, including the assessment and collection of taxes and the more detailed planning of future state revenues. It also produced a much more uniform system for maintaining and auditing accounts; although corruption thrived in Russia, it stood a greater chance of detection than in France, Britain or even the Dutch Republic, where fewer precautions were taken to contain it. A third breakthrough was the creation of a loyal and more productive upper social stratum; the Table of Ranks tied the nobility more effectively to state service than was the case anywhere else in Europe, with the single exception of Prussia. There is therefore much to be said for Massie's overall assessment:

> On balance, Peter's new governmental system was an improvement. Russia was changing, and the Senate and the colleges administered this new state and society more efficiently than would have been possible under the old boyar council and government prikazi.
>
> (Massie 1980: ch. 58)

Some historians extend this line still further. Raeff, for example, writes enthusiastically about the longer-term impact of Peter's reforms:

> Whatever their roots in the past of Muscovy, the reforms of Peter the Great marked the beginning of a new era in Russia's public life. It is hardly an exaggeration to speak of Peter the Great as the founder of the modern Russian state who set the framework of its institutional development for the entire course of the eighteenth and nineteenth centuries.
>
> (Raeff 1966: Introduction)

How accurate is this assessment? Although Peter established the precedent for an effective centralized autocracy, after his death a surprising number of changes was made to the actual institutions he set up. The senate, for example, had a mixed history. Peter's immediate successors, Catherine I (1725–7), Peter II (1727–30) and Anna (1730–40), all ignored it; its place was taken by a privy council which could be seen as a reversion to the *duma*. Elizabeth (1741–62) re-established the senate but it had to compete with an institution known as the *Konferents*. Catherine the Great (1762–96) reduced the senate's powers and ruled through her own imperial council. Eventually Alexander I (1801–25) relegated the senate to a judicial role, and its remaining political functions were absorbed into the council of state. Peter's colleges were also gradually undermined. Between 1725 and 1762 the general tendency was for departmental heads to emerge as petty autocrats, so that, in effect, there was a reversion to the *prikazy* system. Catherine the Great eventually replaced all but three of the colleges with a new system of ministries. The process was continued by Alexander I, who ended the last colleges in 1802 and 1811. Nineteenth-century Russia, therefore, possessed institutions which owed as much to Catherine the Great and Alexander I as to Peter the Great.

Local government and the judiciary

Local government changes were closely connected to those of the central administration. They showed the same general approach: the earlier reforms were piecemeal and improvised, to meet the needs of the moment, while the later ones were more carefully planned.

In order to provide more effectively for the Russian army, Peter subdivided Russia into eight provinces, or military regions, between 1708 and 1710. Known as *gubernii*, these comprised Moscow, St Petersburg, Smolensk, Kiev, Archangel, Kazan, Azov and Siberia. Each was under a governor (*gubernator*) with extensive administrative, judicial, financial and police functions. A second and more systematic set of changes was introduced in 1718 and 1719, coinciding with those in central government. The *gubernii* were subdivided into 50 provinces or counties (*provintsii*), each of which was headed by a military governor (*voevoda*). Within the *provintsii* were several districts (*distrikt* or *uezd*), each administered by a land commissar (*zemskii kommissar*). The whole network was placed under the control of the colleges which, in turn, were subject to the senate.

It has been argued that the inspiration behind these changes was partly the policy of Peter's Romanov predecessors. For example, Michael Romanov had deliberately aimed at extending the influence of central government control by means of the *veovoda*, who was, after all, a traditional Muscovite official. On the other hand, more emphasis is usually given to the importance of western influences and ideas. Realizing that his earlier local government reforms had been relatively unsuccessful, Peter looked to Sweden for inspiration, and was greatly influenced by the detailed analysis of Swedish institutions provided

Government reform.

The Great Embassy

51

for him by Fick. He was tempted by the prospect of transplanting a system which had already proved its worth in sustaining prolonged military campaigns. And the fact that it had been introduced in Sweden at the personal behest of her ruler, Charles XI, made it seem a most attractive precedent for Peter.

Local government faced severe difficulties even after reorganization. The imitation of Swedish system was incomplete since it did not include the lowest unit of Swedish local administration: the parish (*socken*); this was largely because the Russian serfs, unlike the Swedish peasantry, lacked the freedom and experience necessary to participate in local government. This indicates that Peter was less successful in adapting Swedish influences to Russian conditions than has often been maintained. Indeed, Peter rapidly came to the conclusion that his administrative reforms would not work unless the army intervened. Hence further divisions were introduced, based on the regimental district (*polkovoi distrikt*), which overlapped the administrative units or *provintsii*. The army became more and more heavily involved in organizing taxation and the harvesting of resources. This was not even a temporary expedient. Military control was the only form of local administration which worked after Peter's death. The Swedish system gradually evaporated during the reigns of his successors and further attempts at reform were needed, including Catherine the Great's Local Government Statute of 1775.

Was Peter's attempt to change municipal government any more successful? He was certainly ambitious in attempting to introduce western principles as practised in Sweden, Prussia and the Dutch Republic. His 1721 edict ordered each town to set up a council and hold elections on a limited franchise. Municipalities were also given a certain amount of financial responsibility and administrative autonomy. These developments were, however, broadly unsuccessful. Peter had attempted to implant an alien system upon largely traditional communities which lacked any experience of self-government. By the end of his reign failure was already apparent and, as was the case with provincial government, further reforms were necessary in the future, especially Catherine the Great's Municipal Charter of 1785.

Finally, Peter attempted to improve the process of law and order and justice, both at central and at local levels. By the end

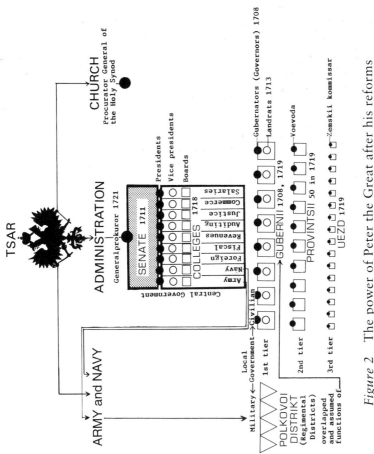

Figure 2   The power of Peter the Great after his reforms

of the reign there were ten court circuits, each with an assize court, while interrogation was conducted, usually under torture by the much feared *preobrazhensky prikaz*, or Secret Chancery. But there was one major omission. Russian law had last been codified in 1649 and had since become lost in a labyrinth of decrees and official orders which prevented uniform application. The only instance of clarification was the Military Statute of 1716, which meant that most of the population lived, in effect, under martial law; this served to reinforce their subjection to military authorities in local government. Peter made three attempts to address the problem but the three commissions of 1700, 1714 and 1720 all failed to produce a new legal code. While he considered codification to be an important component of his 'regulated' state, Peter was too heavily preoccupied with administrative reforms and the demands of war to give it the full attention it deserved. This is therefore the one instance where the conflict with Sweden was an obstacle to, rather than a catalyst for, reform.

The economy

Peter the Great wrote to the senate in 1711 that 'money is the artery of war'. Historians tend to agree that the struggle with Sweden was the key influence behind Peter's various economic reforms. According to E. N. Williams: 'Most of the other transformations that Peter brought about in Russian life stemmed from the necessity of recruiting the men for these forces and raising the revenue for financing the wars they fought' (Williams 1970: ch. 10). The demands were enormous. It has been estimated that over 75 per cent of the revenues were spent on the army and navy in 1701, increasing to 80 per cent in 1710, and falling back to a level of 66 per cent by the end of the reign only when the war was over. As the reign progressed the measures taken to increase the revenues and supply the army exerted an impact on other sectors of the economy. Massie and others believe that this development occurred in two distinct periods – before and after Poltava.

At first, with his country plunged into a major war, Peter's attempt to build industry related entirely to the needs of war. . . . After Poltava, the emphasis changed. As the demands of war diminished, Peter became more interested in other kinds of manufacturing, those designed to raise Russian life to the level of the West and to make Russia less dependent on imports from abroad.

(Massie 1980: ch. 59)

Peter increased the state revenues by two main methods. The first was the introduction of a wide variety of taxes. Many were indirect, falling on items like beards, salt and tobacco. But direct taxes increased even more. Previously these had accounted for about 33 per cent of the total raised by taxation. Peter now raised the proportion to 53 per cent introducing in 1718 a new basic unit called the 'soul' tax, levied on men, women and children. The second method was more of an expedient: the debasement of the currency through the reduction of the silver content and its substitution by base metals. At the same time, the shortage of bullion was partly remedied by edicts preventing the export of silver on pain of death.

In some respects the results of these changes were impressive. Debasing the coinage tided the government over during the first stage of the war with Sweden; it has been estimated that between 1701 and 1709 this produced a total of 4.4 million roubles. Then, after 1718, the yield of direct taxes went up considerably. In its first year, for example, the soul tax produced 4.6 million roubles against the 1.8 million from all other direct taxes used before. The total revenues grew steadily from 3 million roubles in 1701 to 3.3 million in 1710, 7.5 million in 1720 and 8.5 million in 1724. This meant that even after two decades of war the fulfilment of massive schemes such as the construction of a new fleet and the building of a new capital, there were no loans payable to foreign countries. Throughout the reign Peter balanced the budget and raised all funds from domestic sources.

On the other hand, Peter's financial reforms are open to extensive criticism. The fivefold increase in taxation was borne by the long-suffering Russian population. This entirely negated Peter's declared policy of increasing the revenues 'without unduly burdening the people'. It has also been argued that the changes were piecemeal and unsystematic, without, according to Florinsky, 'plan or proper coordination, the various measures, indeed, frequently working at cross-purposes' (1947: ch. 13).

55

The long-term implications were serious. Once the restraining hand of Peter was removed Russia moved into a period of financial turmoil. Both Elizabeth and Catherine the Great raised loans abroad, a practice continued in the nineteenth century.

Peter's industrial policy was constructed on a relatively small base. Although seventeenth-century Muscovy had possessed a number of industries, including a foundry set up at Tula in 1631, these were barely able to compete with the more advanced manufactories of western Europe. At first Peter gave priority to armaments needed in the war with Sweden but, in the second half of the reign, also sought to enlarge and diversify the industrial base by promoting consumer goods such as silk and china. Overall supervision was provided from 1718 onwards by the college of mining and manufacturing, the purpose of which was to generate capital and to promote enterprise, whether individual or state-based.

The results are given unequivocal praise by Anderson, who maintains that 'Of all aspects of Russia's economic life, it was the development of industry which most aroused Peter's interest and in which he achieved most success' (1978: ch. 5). Certainly the increase in production was spectacular. The output of pig iron quadrupled between 1700 and 1720 and the number of manufactories increased from 21 in 1682 to over 200 by 1725; some of these had no equal in Europe in terms of their sheer size. Furthermore, by 1725 over 50 per cent of the value of Russia's exports was in the form of industrial goods. The growth rate was maintained after Peter's death and Russia gradually became Europe's major iron producer in Europe, supplanting Sweden during the reign of Catherine the Great.

There were two major deficiencies in Russian industrial development. One was the comparatively low quality of many goods, such as needles, woollens, silks and linens, manufactured for the domestic market. Much more serious was the lack of success in promoting private enterprise. Some historians have claimed that Peter performed an invaluable service to Russian industry by making available the capital investment which had previously been lacking. Alternatively, it might be argued that this created its own problem as industry became largely dependent on state direction and support. The major difficulties were shortage of capital and backwardness of labour. The sources of capital were really restricted to the nobility and the merchant

56

class, many of whom were unwilling to risk their wealth in uncertain enterprise. Labour was also undermined by the inflexibility of serfdom, which seriously inhibited attempted changes in the future. Thus, although Peter's policies of state control were highly successful at the time, they laid no foundations for the development of private enterprise. Russia never experienced the type of industrial revolution which occurred in Britain or Germany, which depended on entrepreneurial capitalism. Future industrialization depended instead on the sort of periodic state activity which occurred during the reigns of Alexander I and Nicholas II.

Peter showed more interest in agricultural development than has generally been acknowledged. He promoted the cultivation of marginal lands in Siberia, the Volga region and parts of the Ukraine, and also imported Spanish and Silesian breeds to improve the quality of Russian sheep. He secured an overall increase in certain types of produce, including cereals, grapes, hemp, tobacco, flax and wool. His efforts were, however, less obviously successful in agriculture than in industry. His reforming edicts were fragmentary and were not part of an overall coherent policy. He was also confronted by massive resistance to change from a large illiterate peasantry and a nobility which saw no need to change an existing system based on freely available serf labour. Hence traditional methods were still widely used, including the old three-field system with its narrow and isolated strips which were subject to periodic redistribution. The agrarian revolution which, in the late eighteenth century, brought innovations to Britain and western Europe largely bypassed Russia: here the wooden plough was widely used up to the time of the Russian Revolution – and beyond.

Peter's reign saw a considerable increase in Russia's foreign trade. This was not entirely unprecedented since Ivan the Terrible (1533–84) had already established commercial links with England. Peter was also in line with traditional Muscovite policy in pursuing protectionism. At the same time he was also influenced by more distinctively western mercantilist policies; certainly his 1725 tariff raising important duties to an average of 75 per cent was in line with policies elsewhere, even if these were not totally influenced by western economic models. Peter was also open to the influence of western advisers in trying to promote private commercial enterprise to build up a class of entrepreneurs. His 1711 decree, which stipulated that 'people of all ranks may trade in any commodity anywhere' was typical of the liberal economic policy gaining ground in Prussia and the Dutch Republic, as was the relaxation of the state monopoly over foreign trade in 1716. Peter also sought to improve the quality of Russian products by introducing western hybrids such as French vines, Dutch linen manufacturers and German paper-mill technology.

Peter clearly considered the promotion of commerce to be in close harmony with two of his other priorities, which meant that he gave it far more attention than it had ever received before. There was, for example, a natural affinity between overseas trade and his own interest in shipbuilding and nautical matters. Commerce also derived considerable benefit from Russia's new capital. One of Peter's major achievements was to transfer the centre of commercial gravity from Archangel and the White Sea to St Petersburg and the more accessible Baltic. By the end of his reign Russia had increased her foreign exports fourfold, almost all of them going along the internal river and canal network to the new wharves at the mouth of the Neva. Peter's success was not, however, total. As in the case of industry, foreign trade depended very much on government support and initiative and there were still impediments such as insufficient capital and the lack of entrepreneurial skills. Despite his efforts Peter never really succeeded in matching the English and Dutch carrying trade, an indication that Peter was unable to find the resources to equip Russia with a merchant marine as impressive as her navy.

Society, nobility and peasantry

The Russian historian and statesman, Miliukov, argued that Peter 'introduced no social reforms as such'. Instead, the changes affecting the social classes 'were merely the indirect by-products of his legislation, which he himself had least foreseen' (Raeff 1963: p. 33). This section considers the impact of Peter's reign on Russian society in the light of this statement.

It would be inaccurate to claim that Peter did not *attempt* social change. From the earliest years of his reign he was determined to introduce new fashions, based largely on those in the west. His targets included beards and traditional Russian dress, both of which were either banned or heavily taxed. In 1700 and 1702 he issued decrees enforcing Hungarian, French or German dress in urban areas. By 1705 the threat of punishment and fines had resulted in the adoption of western dress by most of the middle and upper classes. Again under western influence, Peter introduced a number of humanitarian measures, endowing Moscow's first pharmacies and hospitals as well as promoting homes for the destitute. On the other hand, these were fairly superficial changes which did not affect the basic fabric of society. Peter had no ambition to revolutionize the traditional Muscovite social structure. His intention was rather to make it more serviceable to the state and hence underpin his other reforms.

The most obvious way in which this might be done was to bring the nobility more directly under the influence of the regime. This had already been attempted by Ivan III (1462–1505) and Ivan the Terrible (1533–84), but efforts had been suspended during the 'time of troubles' (1604–13) and barely resumed by Michael and his seventeenth-century successors. Peter's special contribution to the process was the creation of a new service nobility through his Table of Ranks. His aim was to substitute for the concept of precedence based on ancestral record an emphasis on the importance of actual service to the state. Official positions in the three main branches of state – the army, navy and administration – were divided into fourteen parallel grades or ranks, of which the eighth from the top earned hereditary nobility. While it was conceived within the context of administrative changes, the Table of Ranks should be seen as a reform in its own right and not as a mere 'by-product'. In fact it was possibly the most carefully thought through of all Peter's reforms. It was based on well-tried principles from abroad, especially Charles XI's Disposition of 1696, Christian I's reforms of 1699, and the *Rangordnung* introduced by Frederick William I in 1713. Before opting for these Swedish, Danish and Prussian models, Peter had also ordered a careful examination of the systems in operation in Poland, Venice, Spain and Austria.

The Table of Ranks certainly had a positive impact on the nobility. Official rank within the administration or armed forces now had to be earned: a contrast to the earlier system based on birth and privilege. Service to the state was arduous; it often meant giving up a luxurious lifestyle and could not be abandoned without considerable difficulty. According to Anderson, the Table of Ranks accelerated the 'replacement of the old nobility, proud of its descent and jealous of its privileges, by a new privileged class which reckoned social status essentially in terms of rank in the official hierarchy' (1978: ch. 5). On the other hand, the effects of the new system were limited. The top grades were by and large taken up by the traditional nobility, while the older families kept their aristocratic titles, irrespective of service. There was also no softening of the social hierarchy. The reward for state service was the extension of greater social privileges to the nobility and tightening of their control over the serfs.

The long-term impact of Peter's reforms on the nobility was also very mixed. The Table of Ranks proved remarkably durable, surviving all other changes until the Bolshevik Revolution of 1917. For this reason, argues Florinsky, it has 'a claim to being one of Peter's most lasting reforms' (1974: ch. 15). According to Massie, it survived 'inevitable corrosion by special favours and promotions won by bribes' to remain 'the basis of class structure in the Russian Empire' (Massie 1981: ch. 58). On the negative side, the basic purpose of the Table of Ranks was gradually lost. The bond between the nobility and the state was loosened after Peter's death with the eventual emancipation of the nobility from the harshness of government service. Anna (1730–40) and Elizabeth (1741–62) granted the nobility special privileges, while Peter III introduced his Manifesto Concerning the Freedom of Nobility in 1762, which undid all the reforms of Peter the Great. The Russian nobility became a semi-independent and reactionary barrier to progress, and major reforms of the future sometimes had to be introduced against their unremitting opposition.

How did Peter's reign affect those at the other end of the social spectrum? There were a few measures intended specifically for their benefit. In 1721, for example, a decree was issued to ensure that serfs were sold only as family units, thus preventing the break-up of families which had been all too common in the past. Recognizing that some landlords greatly exceeded their rightful authority, a decree of 1719 stated that a persistently cruel noble might be deprived of his estates. But the overall trend of the reign was the intensification of a longer-term process, described by Lentin as the 'gradual enslavement of a once free peasantry' (1973: ch. 3). Peter contributed significantly to this process.

His main impact was the removal of the different shades of peasantry, some of which had involved degrees of freedom, and to reduce all to one of two categories. These were bonded serfs, belonging to the nobility, and state serfs, employed on crown lands in either agriculture or industry. The latter could be moved around at will or drafted into construction projects such as the building of St Petersburg, which extracted a heavy toll in lives. All serfs were liable to military conscription for periods of up to 25 years – if they survived that long. They were also adversely affected by the introduction of the soul tax in 1718, which imposed a heavy financial burden and increased their dependence on the nobility who supervised their payments. But perhaps the most intolerable measure, and the one most designed to depress the status of the peasantry, was the introduction in 1724 of the passport system as a means of controlling movement between estates and preventing evasion from conscription.

Overall, the social system was subordinate to the interests of the state and therefore related closely to administrative and fiscal change. Peter's reign did, however, produce social measures which are in themselves significant. In the case of the nobility the result was a carefully designed system of service to the state; in the case of the peasantry an increase in exploitation along traditional lines.

Religion and the Church

Peter inherited a tradition of kingship founded firmly in the religious sanction of the Orthodox Church. The Kremlin had been steeped in mysticism, especially during the reigns of Michael (1613–45) and Alexis (1645–76), when the court had had the appearance of a monastery. Peter's attitude was, by contrast, more in keeping with the rationalism of the eighteenth century. Although he believed in a divine being, he had no intention of humbling himself to any earthly representatives. Indeed, his activities with the Most Drunken Synod of Fools and Jesters, which he set up in 1692, showed a degree of contempt for tradition which greatly facilitated his religious changes. These were based on three broad aims. The first was to reduce the influence of the church as a conservative or divisive force. The second was to make more effective use of church resources. Third, and most important, he proposed to integrate the church into his reformed administrative system and thereby underpin his own autocracy.

Peter's intention of cutting the Orthodox Church down to size was not entirely a break with the aims of his predecessors. But his approach was much more radical than theirs had ever been, involving an apparently paradoxical policy of toleration and persecution. Unlike his forebears, Peter allowed different forms of worship; he welcomed Catholic orders like the Franciscans and Capuchins, and legalized marriages and baptisms between different sects. This policy was largely pragmatic, intended to break the spiritual monopoly of the Orthodox Church and encourage the influx of foreigners. 'I intend' he said, 'to imitate Amsterdam in my city of St Petersburg'. The more conservative elements were, however, dealt with firmly, sometimes ruthlessly. Many of the more traditional Orthodox Christians, or Old Believers, tried for religious reasons to evade the changes governing beards and traditional dress. Peter became increasingly exasperated, doubling the soul tax on them and driving many to seek refuge in remote forests to avoid his concept of progress.

Like Ivan III and Ivan IV, Peter also aimed to bring the Church's resources within the orbit of state needs. Unlike them, he succeeded. He diverted an increasingly large proportion of church revenues to secular purposes, including education, alms-houses and the support of disabled soldiers. A particular target were the monasteries. During Peter's reign there were 557 of these, containing 14,000 monks and 10,000 nuns. Some of these were remarkably wealthy, even owning large numbers of serfs. But Peter was scornful of their low literary output and regarded them as parasitic. In 1700, therefore, he placed monasteries under the administration of the newly established Monastery Office which directed and controlled monastic wealth. Peter also decided to dissolve monasteries with fewer than thirty monks and to convert these into schools or parish churches. The larger ones were heavily taxed and ordered to play a more useful role in society. This policy was maintained by Catherine the Great, whose decree of 1764 ordered the closure of most of the larger monasteries, releasing over a million serfs for state service. Both Peter and Catherine therefore adopted the western expedient of transferring part of the wealth of the church to the coffers of the state.

All of Peter's earlier policies led inexorably to the integration of the Church into the administration. On Peter's accession the Church was still dominated by the Patriarchate which had considerable economic wealth and extensive judicial authority. When Patriarch Adrian died in 1700 Peter refused to appoint a successor, despite extensive representations. Instead, the role was filled by a 'Guardian', although the actual administration was conducted by the Monastery Office. Then, towards the end of the Swedish War, Peter began to contemplate a permanent church structure. In 1721 the Ecclesiastical Regulation abolished the Patriarchate and substituted for it the Holy Governing Synod. Based on the model of the administrative colleges, the Synod possessed a president, a vice-president and eight members. These, in turn, came under the authority of the Chief Procurator of the Holy Synod (*Oberprokuror*), who was given equivalent status to the Procurator General of the senate.

There is a consensus among historians that Peter's religious changes were extensive. Raeff, for one, argues that 'of all the reforms of Peter the Great, the abolition of the Patriarchate and the establishment of the Holy Synod was the most radical in form' (1963: p. 45). There is much to justify this view. The Church surrendered its autonomy and the clergy had to swear an oath 'to defend unsparingly all the powers, rights and prerogatives belonging to the High Autocracy of His Majesty'. The ecclesiastical administration was therefore integrated fully into the bureaucracy and subjected to the same regulations and restrictions. This was supplemented by powerful propaganda. Feofan Prokopovich, Archbishop of Novgorod and senior member of the Holy Synod, wrote the 'Right of the Monarchical Will' in 1722 to justify Peter's absolutism. The entire structure remained in force until 1917, including the Church sanction for autocracy. In 1877 the Procurator General of the Holy Synod, Konstantin Pobedonostsev, gave unqualified support to Alexander III: 'The whole secret of Russia's order and progress is above, in the person of the monarch'.

There is less unanimity about the *side-effects* of the ecclesiastical changes. One view is that these were on the whole positive, that Peter opened a new phase in Russian Church history, the so-called Synodal period. Freed from its theocratic constraints, the Church established a more direct contact with and impact on the minds of the people. The result was an increase its membership and a cultural 'upsurge' which implanted a powerful Orthodox influence in Russian literature. The opposite point of view, however, is more popular: the destruction of a traditional relationship brought the total submission of the church to the state. This prevented the church from playing any significant part in the cultural revival; on the contrary, the newly emergent intelligentsia of the mid-nineteenth century were deeply suspicious of the subservience of the church to the tsarist power. Indeed, according to Raeff, the clergy were used by the regime 'as instruments of political repression and control' (in Auty and Obolensky 1976: pp. 147–8). Although there was a religious revival at the end of the eighteenth century, this took place 'largely outside the framework of the church' and the clergy 'became doubly alienated from their flocks'.

Culture

Before Russia could be fully modernized Peter had to promote substantial cultural changes. Some historians believe that he effected a complete transformation. According to Raeff, 'modern Russian culture dates from the 18th century and is intimately related to Peter's reforms' (1963: p. 57). Furthermore, 'The amount of western science and scholarship known in Muscovy at the time of Peter's accession was negligible. The Russians therefore had to learn everything *ab initio*' (in Auty and Obolensky 1976: p. 171).

By contrast, Anderson affirms that 'a far reaching transformation of the intellectual and cultural aspects of Russian life was well under way long before Peter was born' (1978: ch. 5), while it has also been argued believes that there were precedents to the secularisation of Peter the Great which went back far into the seventeenth century, centred on Moscow.

There is, however, a third possibility. Russian culture was a hybrid between traditional Muscovite influences and western implants. The latter had been negligible before the 'time of troubles'. During the seventeenth century, however, western influences penetrated Russia from Poland, which had itself imbibed them from Bohemia and from the German and Italian states. The result was the establishment of the Kiev and Moscow Academies and the extensive introduction of Latin, Greek, Polish and German. On the other hand, westernization was very much a minority movement and traditional Muscovite influences were paramount in literature and all the arts. Peter the Great provided a new and much more powerful impetus. He did this partly by promoting direct contact with French, Dutch, German and English cultures and partly by removing his court from the conservative atmosphere of the Kremlin and establishing a new capital at St Petersburg.

For much of his reign the emphasis was utilitarian, influenced by the demands of war, which meant that priority was given to the languages and sciences, to navigation, shipbuilding and engineering. There were, however, some developments in literature and the arts. The basis was the replacement of the old religious alphabet by the modern 'civil' script and arabic numerals. There was also an admixture of foreign vocabulary which greatly modified the structure of the language and its grammar. The dissemination of foreign literature was assisted by the rapid development of translation and printing; in addition, Peter showed interest in collecting dissertations and having a history of Russia compiled. Meanwhile, Peter promoted western theatre by hiring a company of German players and sponsoring performances of plays of Molière. During the last decade of his reign Peter developed a taste for Italian, Dutch and Flemish paintings, examples of which he acquired from Amsterdam.

The impact of these developments on the future was somewhat mixed. Peter was certainly responsible for secularizing Russian culture and for breaking the stranglehold previously imposed upon it by the Orthodox Church. For this reason Peter had been called the 'father of modern intellectuals'. On the other hand, only a tiny proportion of the population was affected. There was a large gap between a minority of the nobility and upper-middle class in St Petersburg, who adapted to western culture and fashions, and the vast majority of the population. But the size of this westernized élite gradually expanded during the reign of Peter's successors. Elizabeth also did much to promote the fine arts, patronizing the painters like

Vishniakov and Andropov and architects such as Michurin and Ukhtomskii. During the reign of Catherine the Great Russia experienced a renaissance in literature and the arts, and St Petersburg rivalled Paris and Vienna as the cultural capital of Europe. The Russian nobility were to become westernized to such an extent that they adopted French as their main language.

Education

As with culture, Peter's view of education was secular and utilitarian. He considered that the traditional system, dominated by the Church, was incapable of delivering the sort or changes which Peter considered Russia needed as the basis for his proposed transformation. He looked instead to the technical and scientific knowledge of the West, sending selected groups abroad at various stages in his reign. Underlying all his educational reforms was the rapid increase in the availability of translated textbooks, printed in Amsterdam. There was also a proliferation of institutions for training specific skills, usually military or engineering. In 1701 Peter established the School of Mathematics and Navigation, placing it under the guidance of Henry Farquharson, the first of many foreign tutors enticed into Russian service. In the same year the Artillery Academy was founded, followed in 1705 by the Gluck Gymnasium which specialized in politics and western languages, the Engineering Academy (1712), the Naval Academy (1715), the School of Mines (1716) and the Academy of Sciences (1724). These were the first specialist schools in Russian history, but they were not without their problems. Almost all these institutions were for the aristocracy within the military sphere and there was very little for civilians. There was also a low base of student numbers, which meant the eventual closure of the Gluck Gymnasium, and quarrels among organizers which disrupted courses. It therefore took several decades for specialist education to stabilize. The main impetus came during the reign of Elizabeth with the work of Ivan Shuvalov and the foundation of 1755 of Moscow University.

Although a lesser priority, education at the lower levels also made significant progress. Basic literacy and numeracy were taught in elementary or 'cipher' schools, of which there were forty by 1722. Garrison schools were also established during the reign and a decree was issued in 1714 that the *gubernii* should each set up two mathematical schools. The Orthodox Church retained extensive responsibility for the more traditional diocesan schools, although Peter's *Spiritual Regulation* ensured that, in addition to religious knowledge, these taught secular subjects like mathematics, geography, history and philosophy. Most of these institutions used basic textbooks introduced during Peter's reign: a reading primer in 1701, a Russian grammar in 1706, and, in 1703, a textbook on the components of arithmetic, algebra and geometry.

Dukes maintains that 'the professional and primary schools created during the reign of Peter the Great constituted a firm beginning for Russia's educational system' (Dukes 1982: ch. 3). There were, however, serious deficiencies. The different types of establishment struggled to survive in direct competition with each other; the cipher schools were gradually absorbed after Peter's death by the garrison schools, while the mathematical schools fared badly against the parochial schools. More fundamentally, all institutions suffered from insufficient funding and an inadequate supply of teachers. In the final analysis Peter had neither the resources nor the inclination to equip Russia with a broad educational base which might serve eventually to challenge the social structure and even autocracy itself.

Peter the Great's internal reforms: a synthesis

This chapter has considered the domestic policies of Peter the Great from a variety of viewpoints. The final section will attempt to draw together the various themes considered.

Peter's Russia was a state at war. The conflict with Sweden – and, to a lesser extent, that with Turkey – profoundly affected the domestic scene. Since the priority was the effective mobilization of Russian resources to defeat Sweden, institutions had to be examined, overhauled or even replaced. At first the pace was frantic: before 1709 administrative changes were fragmentary and lacked an apparent overall structure. After the victory at Poltava, however, there was more evidence of planning, inspired by western influences. At each stage the impetus came from Peter himself; the war was a catalyst for change largely because he had no deep attachment to Muscovite traditions and was prepared to use any methods to update them. It was this iconoclastic attitude which enabled him to respond positively to the defeat at Narva in 1700 and to convert the prospect of immediate collapse into longer-term revival.

How radical were the changes which helped shape the new regime? One of the purposes of this chapter has been to set Peter's individual reforms within the context of the Muscovite past. These can now be grouped within three general categories.

In the first place, there were a few policies which might be called revolutionary in the sense that they signalled a complete change of direction. They had no precedent in previous reigns beyond the occasional sporadic and swiftly abandoned experiment. One example was the establishment of the navy, which transformed Russia from a land-locked military state into one of Europe's largest naval powers, with nearly 850 warships by 1725. Another was the imposition of state control over the Church, which included the complete overhaul of ecclesiastical administration and the redirection of monastic revenues. More superficially, Peter sought to transform overnight the social fashions and conventions of the middle classes and the nobility through the enforcement of western dress and the shaving of beards, measures which would have been unthinkable during the reigns of his predecessors.

A second category comprises the bulk of Peter's changes: those which had to a certain extent been anticipated in the past but which were now more fully instituted as a result of more conscious imitation of the West. It is sometimes possible to refer to 'revolution' here as well, but in the context of 'acceleration' rather than of a change of direction. A number of Muscovite tsars had, for example, already introduced military reforms or tried out conscription. But it was Peter who increased the size of the army, transformed its infrastructure and equipped it with modern weapons, artillery and training manuals acquired from the west. Similarly, the Muscovite chancelleries (*prikazy*) had already provided an administrative network which, to some extent, Peter streamlined; he did this nevertheless, through the deliberate imitation – down to the last detail – of the Swedish system of colleges, acting on the information systematically gathered between 1716 and 1718 by Heinrich Fick. There had also been certain economic precedents: Ivan the Terrible had sought to open up trading contacts with the West, while the seventeenth century had seen the development of a limited industrial base, especially in the iron works at Tula. Yet it was left to Peter to provide the impetus for sustained rather than sporadic growth. He was heavily influenced by western techniques and theories and sought to transform the Russian economy by an entirely new policy of hybridization. Social trends were also accelerated; Peter succeeded, where his predecessors had failed, in bringing the Russian nobility into state service by means of the Table of Ranks, which was directly influenced by similar developments in Sweden, Denmark and Prussia. Cultural and educational changes were faintly foreshadowed but more boldly etched by Peter in a western image.

At the other end of the spectrum was a third group of policies which were merely a continuation of past trends and which no stretch of the imagination could construe as radical or innovatory. Perhaps the best example was the tightening of the control by the state and the nobility over the serfs and the intensification of the economic and social burdens of the lower orders through the introduction of the soul tax and the extension of conscription for the army and of construction projects.

Another perspective explored by this chapter was the relationship between Peter's changes and the future. Again, a threefold classification might be used.

First, several changes amounted to a radical transformation carried through into future reigns with minimal interruption. The treatment of the Church is perhaps the best example of this. Succumbing entirely to state control, it became in effect a government department; this meant that the ecclesiastical hierarchy underpinned the state power and upheld the principle of Tsarist autocracy. It is difficult to envisage the autocratic power, especially in its last phase, without its religious sanction.

Second, the majority of Peter's reforms can be considered to have had some impact on the future, although with interruption, or modification, or both. The navy, for example, was important in the long term but had to be revived by Catherine the Great after a period of disuse and stagnation during the period from 1725 to 1762. Peter's administration, vital though it was for the development of autocracy, was extensively revised after his death, especially during the reign of Catherine the Great (see p. 50). The Table of Ranks survived as long as imperial Russia itself, although the emancipation of the nobility by Peter III meant that its scope and intentions were heavily diluted. Peter provided a financial and industrial base which enabled Russia to survive as Europe's largest political entity; at the same time, Russia had to struggle constantly with the need to sustain a large military and naval capacity with a limited industrial and entrepreneurial base. Although Peter pushed Russia into an age of industrialization, the whole process had to be repeated at least twice over the next two centuries.

Finally, there were areas in which Peter had no apparent impact on the future and in which his reign therefore made no difference to a longer-term trend. In some instances he chose not to innovate. He considered it totally unnecessary, for example, to change the status of the serfs, preferring to intensify their exploitation as a means of compensating the nobility for increased state service. Alternatively, reforms might be intended, but afforded low priority: as a result there was no legal code, a strange omission for a reign which was otherwise of such importance. Elsewhere he did make the effort to institute changes but failed to have any real impact. Local government was one of the least successful areas in which Peter was involved and experienced the most extensive adaptations in the future. These were necessary largely to remove the military superstructure which Peter had imposed to make it work at all. Despite his attempts to introduce new techniques, Peter also failed to raise the level of agriculture: backwardness, low productivity and wastage were recurrent problems which successive regimes tried, but found it impossible, to address.

4

Peter 'the Great'?

After the signing of the Treaty of Nystadt in 1721, Peter's reputation was confirmed by an oration by Chancellor Golovkin. This concluded:

> ... we take it upon ourselves in the name of the Russian nation and of all ranks of the subjects of Your Majesty, humbly to pray you to be gracious to us and agree, as a small mark of our acknowledgement of the great blessings that you have brought to us and to the whole nation, to take the title: Father of the Fatherland, Peter the Great, Emperor of All Russia.
>
> (Massie 1981: ch. 57)

There were three other examples of near-contemporaries being offered similar titles. The Elector of Brandenburg became the Great Elector after the Battle of Fehrbellin in 1675, while Catherine II and Frederick II were similarly elevated during their reigns. It became fashionable for a while to award the title 'the Great' which had previously been applied to only a handful of historical figures, and then usually in retrospect. Yet even allowing for the consequent devaluation of the currency of 'greatness', there was an awareness throughout Europe that Peter possessed exceptional qualities. In 1724 a British newspaper, not normally given to praising foreign rulers, called him the greatest Monarch of our Age . . . whose Actions will draw after him a Blaze of Glory, and Astonishment, through the latest Depth of Time.

(Anderson 1978: ch. 8)

This concluding chapter will attempt to look beyond the award of a courtesy title by compliant subjects and consider, by examining its components, whether or not it was justifiable.

Greatness is often associated with the grandeur of the monarch's environment. This certainly applies to Louis XIV, who consciously aimed to elevate his image by creating a splendid new court at Versailles and by adopting the motifs of 'le roi soleil' and 'nec pluribus impar'. Peter's court could hardly have formed a greater contrast in the earlier part of his reign, being strictly functional and devoid of trappings. After visiting Versailles in 1717 Peter began to upgrade his courtly image, employing a variety of foreign artists and architects. Even so, his main emphasis was still practical; the most impressive building of the period, constructed by Tressini, housed the senate and colleges, not the court. In one respect, however, Peter's vision was on a far grander scale than Louis XIV's. The French monarch disliked the atmosphere and influence of his capital, and so shifted his court. Peter, on the other hand, broke free from the constraints of his court by building a new capital; the problem of Paris was solved by Versailles, that of the Kremlin by St Petersburg. Peter was also bolder and more confident, taking the unprecedented step of building this capital at the geographical edge of his dominions on territory which had only just been annexed.

Another component of greatness might be the accomplishment of unprecedented changes, perhaps resulting in a new political power base. Peter fell short of the achievements of Lenin here; as Anderson maintains, he 'lacked almost completely the intellectual equipment of a modern revolutionary. He had no ideology, no articulated system of general ideas to guide his actions' (1978: ch. 8). On the other hand, such a comparison might be considered anachronistic. By the standards of the eighteenth century Peter effected a major political transformation. He grafted on to traditional Muscovite autocracy a more effective administration, inspired by western example. The supreme power of the person of the tsar was now underpinned by a complex bureaucracy. Together these comprised what has been called a 'leviathan state', the eighteenth-century equivalent of the modern authoritarian regime.

Of course, power should be assessed qualitatively as well as quantitatively. We have seen in Chapter 3 that Peter used his power to introduce a series of military, political, social, economic and educational reforms. Pushkin considered these evidence that he used his authority as a benefactor rather than as a tyrant:

> With an autocratic hand
> He daringly sowed enlightenment.
> (Pushkin 1826: *Stances*)

This eulogy would place him firmly within the context of the eighteenth-century Enlightened Despots, a group of monarchs who believed that it was within their means to create a better political and social system by applying the basic precepts of the intellectual movement known as the Enlightenment. Frederick the Great, for example stated that 'A well conducted government must have a system as coherent as a system of philosophy'. Other rulers with whom Enlightened Despotism is generally associated are Catherine the Great (1762–96), Joseph II (1780–90), Leopold of Tuscany and Charles Frederick of Baden. Most historians would, however, exclude Peter the Great from this list, on the grounds that he was not directly influenced by the Enlightenment and that his reforms were introduced as a result of immediate necessity rather than as part of a rational plan. It could also be argued that Peter was not an Enlightened Despot because, rather than aspiring to be a 'philosopher king', he always considered himself an 'artisan tsar'. This inevitably meant that his reforms had limitations. As Ivan Betskii told Catherine the Great in 1767: 'Peter the Great created men in Russia; Your Highness has given them souls' (Riasanovsky 1985: ch. 1).

Some would consider popularity an important feature of 'greatness'. This Peter clearly lacked. Indeed, a considerable degree of opposition developed which, according to Cracraft, 'was both constant and pervasive'. This was demonstrated by the records of the *Preobrazhenskii Prikaz*, which indicated that 'political offenses were committed by persons of every rank and social condition' so that 'Peter I faced by 1708 a kind of national resistance'. The more traditional clergy saw Peter as the Antichrist, while in the Church at large there was extensive distrust of his anti-clerical measures and secularization. The traditional nobility were alienated by the introduction of state service, by the cost of the war with Sweden, and by the apparent futility of westernization. There were numerous, if isolated, revolts by peasants against the extra tax burdens imposed upon them and the depression of their social status, while Lefort recorded in 1723 that poverty was so severe that 'the streets are full of people who try to sell their children'. There was, however, an alternative perspective. Some, like Ivan Pososhov (an economic adviser), saw Peter as an heroic figure struggling against ingrained backwardness and suspicion: 'The Tsar pulls uphill with the strength of ten, but millions pull downhill.' Peter also tended to see himself in this role, justifying any harsh policies accordingly: 'Though a thing be good and necessary, yet if it be new, our people will not do it unless forced to.'

Peter cannot by any stretch of the imagination be placed among the short list of rulers generally held to have shown military genius. He entirely lacked the timing and finesse of Napoleon at Austerlitz in 1805, nor was he able to come up with a new tactic such as the linear formation employed by Gustavus Adolphus at Breitenfeld (1632) or the oblique attack which enabled Frederick the Great to defeat a numerically greater Austrian army at Leuthen in 1757. On the other hand, no ruler knew better how to survive military defeat and make effective use of his country's terrain and climate. His calculated withdrawal before Charles XII, which culminated in the Russian victory at Poltava in 1709, also provided inspiration in similar circumstances in the future – particularly to Kutuzov against Napoleon in 1812 and Marshal Zhukov from 1942 onwards.

Territorial aggrandizement would certainly have been regarded as an essential part of any eighteenth-century concept of 'greatness'. In Peter's case, however, this might be misleading. The amount of territory he actually annexed during his reign was not extensive, amounting to the littoral of the eastern Baltic, the southern shore of the Caspian Sea and the remote peninsula of Kamchatka. These gains compare unfavourably with the rapid spread of Russian rule across Siberia in the seventeenth century or with the incorporation by Catherine the Great of large portions of the Ottoman Empire and Poland. Yet the importance of Peter's Baltic additions cannot be overstated.

It was the most significant conquest in Russia's entire history, accompanied as it was by the establishment of a new capital – and a new outlook. Without this key territory Russia could not have become a European power and certainly could not have developed the naval capacity which was soon to become second only to Britain's.

Underlying all of Peter's achievements was a frantic energy and a phenomenal will-power shown by no other ruler (with the possible exception of Napoleon I). He involved himself in every facet of Russian development and considered nothing to be unworthy of his attention. Frederick the Great showed a similar all-embracing interest, but the scale of the demands on him was entirely different: Prussia was far less than 1 per cent the size of Russia and had less than 10 per cent of the latter's population. Peter owed his achievements less to innate brilliance than to sheer perseverance which produced amazing results from an apparently unpromising combination of mediocrity and eccentricity. He once observed that 'Without loss of a single instant, we devote all our energies to work'. His activity became legendary. Lomonosov, an eighteenth-century scientist, said: 'I see him everywhere, now enveloped in a cloud of dust, of smoke, of flame, now bathed in sweat at the end of strenuous toil. I refuse to believe that there was but one Peter and not several' (Massie 1981: Epilogue). The nineteenth-century poet, Pushkin, described Peter as the 'eternal toiler upon the throne of Russia'.

The true test of 'greatness' is time. For nearly three centuries Peter has consistently been seen as one of the main focal points of Russian and European history. At first he was the subject of a cult, started deliberately during his lifetime by Feofan Prokopovich and sustained after his death by the poet Derzhavin who asked, extravagantly, 'Was it not God Who in his person came down to earth?' Catherine the Great took care to project her policies as a continuation of his. Up to the end of the eighteenth century the reaction to Peter was uniformly favourable. During the nineteenth century, however, views began to polarize. At one extreme, he was seen by the Westernizers as the source of all that was civilized and progressive in Russian development. At the other, he was anathema to the Slavophiles, who blamed Peter for uprooting Russia's traditions and for committing unprecedented violence on her institutions and culture (see p. 39). As the nineteenth century progressed the attitudes to Peter became more complex as the debate on his role intensified. The Westernizers developed a splinter group who considered that, while Peter had introduced western influences, he had also developed in the leviathan state institutions which were incompatible with aspirations for democracy which were then being harboured by Russian liberals. After the Bolsheviks seized power in October 1917, Peter retained the sharp focus he had always received, although the attitude to him became even more ambivalent. He was portrayed, on the one hand, as the ultimate representative of a westernized system which exploited the labouring classes, and, on the other, as one of the great heroes of Russian history. Stalin was partly responsible for his rehabilitation, seeing him as a useful rallying point during the 'Great Patriotic War' against Nazi Germany.

The impact of Peter the Great on the Russian imagination is therefore unbroken, his only serious rival being Lenin. Like Peter, Lenin's reputation was launched by the creation of a personality cult. But Lenin's cult was destroyed by the collapse of the ideology to which it was tied. This means that Peter has now re-emerged as the key figure in Russian history, a point given special symbolic significance in 1991 by the restoration to Leningrad of its original name, St Petersburg.

Select bibliography

Primary sources included in:
B. Dmytryshyn (1974) (ed.) *Imperial Russia: A Source Book, 1700–1917* (Hinsdale, Ill.).
L.J. Oliva (1970) (ed.) *Peter the Great* (Englewood Cliffs, N.J.).

Secondary sources

General histories

E. Auty and D. Obolensky (1976) (eds) *An Introduction to Russian History* (Cambridge).
P. Dukes (1974) *A History of Russia* (London).
W. and A. Durant (1963) *The Story of Civilization: The age of Louis XIV* (New York).
M.T. Florinsky (1947) *Russia: A History and an Interpretation* (New York), Vol. 1.
M.S. Lentin (1973) *Russia in the Eighteenth Century* (London).
M. Rady (1990) *Russia, Poland and the Ukraine 1462–1725* (London).
B.H. Sumner (1944) *Survey of Russian History* (London).
E.N. Williams (1970) *The Ancien Regime in Europe 1648–1789* (London).

Biographies

M.S. Anderson (1978) *Peter the Great* (London).

I. Grey (1962) *Peter the Great* (London).

V. Klyuchevsky (1958) *Peter the Great* (English edn, London).

R.K. Massie (1981) *Peter the Great* (London).

B.H. Sumner (1950) *Peter the Great and the Emergence of Russia* (London).

Issues

B. Dmytryshyn (ed.) (1974) *Modernization of Russia under Peter I and Catherine II* (New York)

P. Dukes (1982) *The Making of Russian Absolutism 1613–1801* (London).

E. Mendelsohn and M. S. Shatz (eds.) (1988) *Imperial Russia 1700–1917; Essays in Honour of Marc Raeff* DeKalb, I11. Especially J. Cracraft, 'Opposition to Peter the Great'.

R. Nisbet Bain (1897) *The Pupils of Peter the Great* (Westminster).

C. Peterson (1979) *Peter the Great's Administrative and Judicial Reforms; Swedish Antecedents and the Process of Reception* (Stockholm).

M. Raeff (1963) (ed.) *Peter the Great: Reformer or Revolutionary?* (Boston, Mass.).

—— (1966) *Plans for Political Reform in Imperial Russia, 1730–1905* (Englewood Cliffs, N. J.).

N.V. Riasanovsky (1985) *The Image of Peter the Great in Russian History and Thought* (New York).

G.L. Yaney (1973) *The Systematization of Russian Government* (Chicago).